How To Build a Traditional
FORD HOT ROD

REVISED EDITION

Mike Bishop and Vern Tardel

Illustrations by Steve Amos

 Publishing Company

First published in 2000 by MBI Publishing Company, 729 Prospect Avenue, PO Box 1, Osceola, WI 54020-0001 USA

MBI Publishing Company books are also available at discounts in bulk quantity for industrial or sales-promotional use. For details write to Special Sales Manager at Motorbooks International Wholesalers & Distributors, 729 Prospect Avenue, PO Box 1, Osceola, WI 54020-0001 USA.

Library of Congress Cataloging-in-Publication Data Available
ISBN 0-7603-0900-0

On the front cover: The finished Bishop-Tardel roadster is a timeless hot rod combination, a '29 Model A high-boy with a Ford flathead V-8. And this one's built just as it would've been done in the early 1950s, with all early Ford parts.

On the back cover: The Bishop-Tardel roadster as it was nearing completion in Vern Tardel's shop. At this point, the car is far enough along that you can envision the finished product . . . the roadster needs only a comfortable—and attractive—interior to be a complete, first-rate traditional hot rod.

At home in the blue roadster's engine bay, the fully dressed flathead is the definitive hot rod motivator. This example is a ported 1946 Ford 59A block with a 1949 Mercury 4-inch crank and rods, Egge pistons, and an Isky 400 Jr. cam with Johnson adjustable tappets.

Edited by Steve Hendrickson
Text Design by Terry Webster
Cover Design by Jim Snyder

Printed in the United States of America

Contents

Preface _____ 4

Acknowledgments _____ 5

Introduction _____ 6

The Definitive Ford Hot Rod
Chapter 1 _____ 9

Frame
Chapter 2 _____ 25

Front Suspension and Steering
Chapter 3 _____ 35

Rear Suspension, Axle, and Driveline
Chapter 4 _____ 46

Brakes, Wheels, and Tires
Chapter 5 _____ 58

Engine
Chapter 6 _____ 69

Transmission
Chapter 7 _____ 81

Body and Paint
Chapter 8 _____ 86

Controls and Instruments
Chapter 9 _____ 101

Fuel System
Chapter 10 _____ 108

Electrical
Chapter 11 _____ 119

Bells and Whistles
Chapter 12 _____ 124

Interior and Top
Chapter 13 _____ 138

One Year Later (Epilogue)
Chapter 14 _____ 143

Appendix A
Parts and Information Sources _____ 151

Appendix B
Bishop-Tardell 1929 Ford Roadster Specs _____ 156

Ford Flathead Engine Tuning _____ 157

Index _____ 158

Preface

Believe it or not, there was a time in post-World War II America when there were no Chevy small blocks, no Ford 9-inch rear ends, nor Turbo 350 transmissions. Yet in spite of this dearth of today's building blocks, the right stuff, hot-rodders managed to put together some nifty rides.

The situation then wasn't really so different from what it is now. There was a lot of good, affordable hardware around that could be adapted to build strong-running, long-lasting hot rods. It was just different hardware than we work with today. Then, like now, rodders had to know which pieces were the right ones and how to make them work. For this knowledge, they turned to older brothers or friends, and in rare cases their fathers. We say "rare" because in those days, hot-rodding wasn't a family activity. It was something you were supposed to outgrow, which is what most fathers had done by the time their sons were old enough to be interested in hot rods.

Good information was also available in the fledgling automotive press. Of the several rodding monthlies, *Hot Rod* magazine was the mainstay with its detailed how-to articles and state-of-the-art technical analyses. *Hot Rod*, in concert with the National Hot Rod Association (NHRA) and the Southern California Timing Association (SCTA), defined and codified hot-rodding, legitimizing it as sport, hobby, and industry.

The postwar era is widely regarded as hot-rodding's finest time— its Golden Age. In this prosperous period, hot-roddable Fords were inexpensive and a burgeoning speed equipment industry rushed to fill the needs of an eager market. Experimentation and innovation formed the energy that fueled this movement. While before the war hot-rodding was a make-do affair, it was now approached from a what-if mindset. The young adult hot-rodders also had the wherewithal and the essential skills (learned in the military) to pursue their best ideas with style.

The hot rods of that era are as appealing today as they've ever been, and all for the same and very right reasons, not the least of which is their cost— $5,000 to $20,000 today depending on your bargaining and building skills. The cost of constructing a present-tech street rod from available aftermarket hardware has risen steadily in recent years, until now even the simplest highboy roadster has a hardware ticket of around $20,000. Add paint, plating, and upholstery and the cost jumps to around $30,000—assuming the owner does most of the work.

Even a simple, home-built fat-fendered car will cost $15,000 to $25,000, depending on how good the body is to start with. And this doesn't include a top chop, which can raise the ante another $5,000 for an easy chop!

Not surprisingly, a great many "resto-rods" from the 1970s are being dusted off and retro-fitted with solid wheels for a more traditional 1950s look. Still, even a marginally desirable resto-rod will fetch $12,000–$15,000 before it's been returned to a traditional style. And underneath, it will probably consist of a small block Chevy, an automatic transmission, and a contemporary Ford or Chevy rear end. So much for tradition.

For many, however, a retro re-do doesn't stop at cosmetics but will also include an engine reswap to a very early Cadillac or Oldsmobile OHV V-8, a handsome Buick "nailhead," or a formidable Hemi from Chrysler. And again, the ante is increased, making a fundamental all-the-way-back, all-Ford hot rod even more appealing in its affordability.

Acknowledgments

Like all good hot rods, mine was built with the often eager assistance of a great many hot-rodders to whom I owe an incalculable debt. My partner in this adventure, Vern Tardel, heads the list, because without Vern's knowledge, experience, creativity, skills, perseverance, contacts, and wonderful parts pile, the Bishop-Tardel Highboy wouldn't have happened.

Another key and invaluable player, involved from the beginning and on through the duration, is Bill Grainger, an excellent painter and metalman whose 110 percent effort is largely responsible for the blue car's crisp appearance. Bill's also a special friend whose sense of humor kept us smiling throughout, and was often responsible for poking vent holes in egos that were in danger of exploding. Nobody gets away with anything when Bill's around.

Here, with cogent attributions, are the rest of those who made it all work:

Ed Binggeli—*NorCal's flatheader emeritus who hasn't forgotten any go-fast trick he's ever learned, and willingly shares them.*

Stan Vermiel—*Automotive arts teaching pro and machinist extraordinaire.*

Charlie Brown—*Our favorite publican and a wicked man with a grinder.*

Gary Henshaw—*A most crafty fellow, destined to be the first man to make a TIG torch talk.*

Terry Schank—*A clever metal shaper and stitcher of the first order.*

Bobby Johnson—*Exhaust specialist with a bracket, hanger, or solution for any application you can imagine.*

Jack Buchanan—*A talented young trimmer who does tuck-and-roll like the old-timers.*

Doug Day—*His brake plumbing is as handsome as it is perfect. Not so much as a hint of a leak anywhere.*

Terry Griffith—*Electrical wizard and ace wireman, whose unobtrusive work all but disappears.*

Gene Hutchinson—*Veteran plater and polisher, who gave us correct old-Ford finishes that most folks have forgotten about.*

John Clapham—*Inspiration, pep talks, and a sand-blasting unit that removed decades of rust and scale in an afternoon when it all began.*

John Castetter—*For John, the devil is in the detailing.*

Gary Camara—*Persistent and patient, a good pal to help with last-minute stuff.*

Patrick Dykes—*First-rate flathead shopkeeper who got behind us right from the start.*

Tim Love—*The man who helped us put some dash in the cockpit.*

Rod Powell—*It was with great restraint that he provided subtle, old-Ford style striping.*

Don Montgomery—*Author and major keeper of the flame, whose great books served as both inspiration and reference, and who graciously allowed us to use many historic photos from his archives.*

Vance Lausmann—*Pro communicator and past project partner who made sure the words and pictures wound up where they belonged, looking good as well.*

Bill Williams—*My best pal since we were kids, all-time favorite co-conspirator, and the one responsible for the original roadster start that inspired this one.*

This is hardly a definitive list; you'll find more contributors in the Appendix, where we've gathered the names, addresses, and phone numbers of the people and organizations that consistently provide the hardware and services with which old Ford hot rods are built.

I also acknowledge my hot-rodding heroes, men who have inspired me since I was 12 years old. No elaboration or explanations are needed; their names will suffice: Wally Parks, Tom Medley, Don Ferrara, and Dave Mitchell.

Finally, I extend a very special thank you to Steve Amos, whose wonderful illustrations make this book extra special. I have no doubt that Xerox blowups of many of them will find their way onto shop and office walls.

INTRODUCTION

Like folk tales and legends, hot rod building intelligence is part of the lore of the tribe—the shared common body of knowledge that's passed from one person to the next. But when the tribe gets a better idea, the telling of the old ways begins to fade because everyone's talking about the new stuff. In time, the old ways are all but forgotten, practiced and preserved by only a handful of elders who understand the significance and importance of those ways. These are the keepers of the flame of tradition.

With great assistance from several keepers of the hot-rodding flame, this book was written to relate the old ways and thus ensure the perpetuation of the tradition through the passing of the torch.

My original roadster was beginning to take shape when this picture was taken in 1954. The rear cross-member had been stepped, the cowl had been filled, new Goodyear Super Eagles covered a pair of temporary old Ford spokers, the two-dollar axle needed only a little correction as did the too-tall Deuce radiator, and there were two perfect 1934 torque tube housings sitting inside, ready to be turned into "lakes pipes." Even at this stage the stance was already pretty good, and it sat about 8 inches lower than the stock-height Model A sitting next to it.

A dozen years ago I began formulating a plan to resurrect a dream from my early teens—to build a highboy roadster like those that decorated the pages of *Hot Rod* magazine in the early 1950s. By the time I was 16 years old, in 1954, I had advanced the dream well along the way toward reality, collecting most of the essential pieces for the actual hot rod that cruised and raced in my imagination.

My original plan was very specific, based on a particular roadster that had captured my heart from the moment I first saw it in HRM. Built by a fellow named Don Ferrara, it was the quintessential A-V8 highboy, a fenderless Model A roadster fitted with a flathead Ford V-8 motor, lightweight and nimble, powerful, and stunningly handsome.

The basic package, a 1929 roadster started by my best friend, Bill Williams, fell into my hands when Bill's family moved to Los Angeles and the unfinished roadster was not on the Bekins manifest. Not quite two years later, when my family moved to SoCal, I in turn surrendered the roadster—still unfinished and with many important flathead hot-rodding lessons yet to be learned—to a couple of pals for 50 bucks, which they would mail to me as soon as they had it. That check's been in the mail for a long time.

Like a lot of gearheads my age I was caught up in the excitement generated by the hot new V-8 from sensible old Chevrolet. Shortly after I graduated from high school I began an association with the Bowtie that will probably endure to the end of my days. So, when I started thinking about that unfinished roadster a dozen years ago it was logical that I would amend my plan to use a small-block Chevy, which I knew intimately, in place of a Ford flathead V-8, which still held some mysteries for me.

Before the new roadster project was launched, however, I moved to northern California and became immersed in the local hot-rodding scene, one in which flatheads still played a major role. It was here I met Vern Tardel, a key figure in the group of NorCal flatmotor adherents and a near-life-long practitioner of old Ford hot rod construction. For Vern, building old Ford-based hot rods isn't just fun, it's also his livelihood, with the work conducted in a shop reminiscent of small-town, full-service, automobile repair shops, as they were about midcentury.

Vern and I became acquainted during the course of writing and illustrating stories about his work. I found his traditional approach to rod building to be particularly interesting as did the readers of a magazine for which I was writing. At a time when other professional rod builders are constructing cars with a mix-and-match arrangement of old and new technology supplemented with many modern bits and pieces from the current aftermarket, Vern builds hot rods just as they were built in immediate post-World War II America, with parts from the pool that existed at that time.

The exposure to the traditional-style cars, along with the sound flathead technology I was finally learning well enough to pass along to others, had rekindled my interest in my roadster project. This time it would go all the way back to its original iteration, however—90 percent Ford content and flathead powered.

That there was enough information involved to fill a book was obvious. Also obvious was that unless one had access to someone like Vern, the information for building a traditional Ford hot rod involved a long and often fruitless search through decades-old magazines to find the hows and whys . Even so, much of the information needed had never been committed to print but instead was passed along between generations of hot-rodders.

Vern was receptive to the idea of helping me create a book that would follow the car's construction from start to finish. The uncompromised authenticity in Vern's cars stems from an abiding interest in the genesis of the hot rod and an almost reverential respect for the movement's pioneers. Here was an opportunity for Vern to pass along the traditional technology that his mentors had shared with him over the years—a way for him to put something back into hot-rodding. For me, it was an excellent opportunity to learn those lessons that eluded me in my teens and to also repay the movement that had kept me entertained for most of my life, by sharing those lessons with others in words and pictures. The project would span three years, from first plan to published book. Building the car took nearly two years because it had to be fitted in around the paid work in Vern's shop.

Although the bulk of the work described in the book covers the buildup of one specific hot rod, options are presented for most areas of construction.

While I chose a Model A frame as a platform because that was what I had under my original car, we also describe the construction of a Deuce-framed chassis. Several schemes for front axle control are described, as are different brake types, and the use of a new 1929 Ford roadster body doesn't rule out the use of old tin or even a roadster pickup, coupe, or sedan. For that matter, it's no stretch to apply the techniques and technology you'll find here to building an all-'32 highboy. Such is the nature of hot rod construction.

This book is not so much a blueprint as it is a menu, designed to provide you with the informational foundation that would have been readily available to you in the early 1950s, just for the asking. We endeavored also to provide you with the courage to undertake building a hot rod made of pieces that are far less common today than they were five decades ago but are still available. Most important, we share the fun and satisfaction that comes from reconfiguring old Ford hardware into traditional hot rods.

Flash forward 45 years to when the dream is realized. Following a couple of years on the road, and approaching 20,000 miles, it just continues to get better.

Chapter 1

THE DEFINITIVE FORD HOT ROD

The most enduring image of a traditional hot rod is a flathead-powered highboy Ford roadster, fenderless, usually black or some other dark color, with a slight windshield chop, and Ford disc wheels with chrome hubcaps and stainless steel trim rings. There was far more diversity to hot-rodding in the post-World War II period, of course, and even in sunny southern California, coupes were nearly as popular. But none were as treasured as a highboy roadster—the archetypal, definitive, open-wheel Ford hot rod.

Just as all hot rods weren't highboy roadsters, neither were they all Fords, although non-Ford hot rods were a small minority up through the early postwar period. The popularity of Ford roadsters, mostly Model As and '32s with a sprinkling of Model T bodies mounted on A and Deuce chassis, was partly practical in that they performed well even when stock, they were simple and sturdy, and they were cheap. But most important, they looked great!

Don Ferrara's pure A-V8 was one of the very best of its time and style. Featured in *Hot Rod* magazine in May 1950 and on the cover in August 1951, the red highboy was constructed in the 1940s with a built 21-stud motor and was a dry lakes racer as well as transportation. Plated 1937 spring-in-front suspension, elegant exhaust system, and high level of quality throughout made the car a standout. It was featured in *HRM* again in August 1953, then owned by Bill Rolland, with a 1948 Mercury motor, 1953 Ford taillights in place of the 1950 Pontiac illumination, and white lacquer. *Don Ferrara*

Don Ferrara's A-V8.

Dave Mitchell's shop truck.

A PRACTICAL HOT ROD APPROACH

We've taken a very practical hot-rodding approach in this book, confining it to the build-up of a single, specific Ford hot rod—an A-V8 highboy roadster. The designation is as simple as the car it describes—a Model A with a flathead V-8. A complete 1932 chassis and drivetrain with a 1928–1929 roadster body—one of hot-rodding's most desirable combinations—is not a true A-V8 in the strictest sense, although it's often referred to as such; the designation originally referred to the chassis and body, not just the body. Because of the popularity of the Deuce chassis and availability of new original style frame rails, however, we've included the 1932 frame as an alternate platform, with the information and dimensions necessary to make it fit the Model A body.

The A-V8 was an inevitable hybrid of the time; not only were Model As cheap, plentiful, and lighter than '32s, many had already been rodded in the 1930s with hopped-up four bangers. The upgrade to a V-8 was a relatively simple and very logical engine swap.

And when the job was done correctly, incorporating a complete 1932 frame K-member, the flexible Model A ladder frame settled down rather nicely to its increased performance duties.

The A-V8 is an excellent traditional rod to build today because virtually everything required is available, including brand spanking new steel bodies, thanks to an old and well-established restoration parts industry. Used original and New Old Stock (NOS) parts—original parts that have never been on a car—still show up after being squirreled away years ago by restoration hobbyists who just knew the stuff would be needed in the future.

NINETY PERCENT FORD CONTENT

A Model A needed some help to become an A-V8 hot rod, aside from the flathead V-8. The hot-rodder of the 1940s and 1950s seldom looked beyond the hulks in wrecking yards or the bins in the local Ford dealer's parts department for everything that was required, however, because traditional Ford hot rods were based almost entirely on early Ford components—about 90 percent Ford content in most cases.

While wrecking yards are just about out of old Ford parts today, and dealers haven't stocked the right stuff for several decades, it's still possible to build a 90 percent Ford hot rod. The parts hunt just takes a little longer now.

There's a handsome reward for your effort in that a traditional 90 percent Ford A-V8

Dave Mitchell's shop truck—a 1929 A-V8 roadster pickup with a touring car bustle grafted to the back of the cab. Initially flathead powered, the handsome truck later received an Olds V-8, wide whites, and Fiesta wheel covers in keeping with the trend of the time. The outstanding external lakes pipes showcased Mitchell's expert exhaust system work. *Dr. Bob Atol*

The late Larry Shinoda may have designed the Corvette Stingray, but he wasn't always a Chevy man. His simple A-V8 roadster pickup was pure postwar SoCal Ford hot rod—fenderless, hot flathead mill, and a Deuce grille between independently mounted headlights. *Don Zabel*

highboy roadster can be put together for 50 to 60 percent of the cost of a present-tech street rod. In addition, when correctly and carefully built, the traditional car, even with all of its outdated technology, will be worth as much or more than a current-tech car of the same quality, built from expensive repro aftermarket pieces.

But the big payoff isn't so much in the savings as it is in the satisfaction of creating a hot rod the way hot rods were built in the past—almost entirely from genuine Ford parts and with lots of sweat equity.

WHERE DO WE GET ALL THE OLD FORD HARDWARE?
As you set out to gather the pieces for your Ford hot rod, forget about most of the sources for street rod parts; they have little or nothing you'll need for your traditional hot rod. Instead, write or call each of the suppliers shown in Appendix A at the back of the book and collect their current catalogs and literature.

The folks listed have a lot of what you'll need, but some of the hardware for your hot rod is out of 800 number/plastic-card range. You're going to have to get seriously involved and do some leg work.

NHRA's founder and chairman, Wally Parks, was editor of *Hot Rod* magazine in the early 1950s when he was shown in his 1932-framed A-V8 at the beginning of his editor's column each month.

Bob Bennett's very tidy pure A-V8 served him both at the lakes (129.12 miles per hour) and on the street as daily transportation in 1949. Note the full tonneau, useable for cool-weather driving with the windshield in place. Note also the neat track roadster style nerf bar. *Dan O'Regan*

The best source for old Ford hardware is the growing body of new street rodders. Think of them as "parts farmers." They're harvesting a lot of the hardware you need for your traditional hot rod. They take perfectly good pieces—often completely rebuilt—off old Fords and replace them with popular in-vogue hardware. Thanks to street rodding, there's a huge pool of hot rod makings at swap meets and bargain-hunter newspapers like the *Penny-Saver* and *Recycler*.

Another great source for parts is the local chapter of the national Ford Early V-8 Club. While some members are hard-core preservationists, many enjoy Ford-based hot rods right along with their restored cars. It's not uncommon to find restored and hot-rodded Fords sharing space in members' garages. Plug in to the right group, and you'll find yourself with all the old Ford hardware you need, along with some interesting new friends. Just as important, you'll have tapped an invaluable source of technical information about old Ford components.

BOILOVERS, BROKEN AXLES, AND OTHER FORD MYTHS

We all know how bad those old Ford hot rods were, don't we? So why would we want to create another one? Well, if they really were fundamentally bad cars we wouldn't even be thinking about building one, nor would have the countless hot-rodders who built them in the past and continue to build them today. Affordable Fords weren't the only cars available, but they offered the greatest potential for a hot-rodder's effort and money at the time.

Even so, many young builders never realized that potential, just as inexperienced rodders today miss the target when they take a perfectly good pile of the latest parts and create a weak-running, poor-handling car that's just as wrong as it can be. Then as now, the blame is placed squarely on the hardware, and old Ford hardware garnered far more than its share of bad publicity.

What gave legs to the old Ford myth, and at least a veneer of truth, was that the myth was built mostly on first- and second-hand experience. But those legs buckle when we consider that most of the experiences were those of highly inexperienced young hobbyists, many of whom simply gave up on flatheads out of frustration. They just never stuck around long enough to learn how to build them correctly.

So, let's look at the complaints and problems that make up the myths about old Ford hot rods and see if they really were so bad after all.

Overheating—"*All Ford flatheads overheat and there's nothing you can do about it; that's just they way they are.*"

This one is more than myth. It belongs in the list of Greatest Lies, right along with "The check's in the mail." Ford flatheads can be made to overheat, just as easily as any other engine can, and easier than some. There's even merit in arguments based on the long exhaust tracts that run through the water jackets. It's also true that large overbores run hot, but that's the case with most overbored engines. The reality is that these factors only exacerbate engine-building ignorance and sloppiness, which are the true causes for overheating and the myth that attends it.

The "secrets" for building a cool-running flathead are no different today than they were in the past. If you are one of the strugglers of old who's gained some maturity over the years, you'll enjoy the lessons and hints in Chapter Six. If you're convinced, however, that you had all the answers back then and still couldn't make those damn Fords run cool, stick with us and give us a chance to change your mind.

Driveline breakage—"*Ford transmissions are hand grenades just waiting for someone to pull the pin. They're almost as bad as those keyed axles that break like glass.*"

In good condition, an old Ford V-8 transmission is up to the task of handling a strong-running flathead, so long as it's treated sensibly. True, you can't rush your shifts the way you can with a Muncie "rockcrusher," nor does the Ford gearbox hold up very long to side-stepping the clutch with the motor at three grand. But when carefully assembled with good parts (see chapter seven) and treated with a bit of discretion, the Ford three-speed is an altogether decent transmission.

Old Ford keyed axles have taken about as much verbal abuse as they have physical punishment through the years, neither of which they've earned. The common culprit here is a loose axle nut—a product of incorrect assembly. The axle nuts require about 150 to170 foot-pounds of tightening torque, and when rear brake drums are removed for brake work, the uninitiated do-it-yourselfer invariably settles for a whole lot less when he puts it all back together. As a result, the drums move ever-so-slightly as the car is driven, working away at the key and the axle until one or the other gives up.

Poor brakes—"*Old Ford brakes are terrible. They lock up a different wheel each time you jump on them, and when you use them a lot they fade and just won't stop safely.*"

Omitting the obvious—mechanical brakes—and moving on to 1939 to 1948 Ford hydraulics, the quarrel once again is mostly with the maintainer, although we agree that Ford-design hydraulic brakes were not the best. Perhaps we should be thankful that old Henry relented on

Mark Smith's pure A-V8 got its low-for-1947 stance from a mild axle drop and a radical frame step in the rear. In El Mirage livery—minus headlights and windshield—the neat little daily driver recorded 121-plus mph. *Mark Smith*

the mechanical vs. hydraulic issue at all, even though the Ford design was not nearly as effective as the prevailing Bendix design, for which Henry would have had to pay licensing fees—something that was totally foreign to his rather parsimonious nature. Suffice to say that with careful and frequent adjustment, Ford brakes work acceptably well, although they require more pedal pressure than Bendix brakes.

The best avenue for the builder of a traditional Ford hot rod today is the one taken by hot-rodders in the 1940s and 1950s—a switch to hydraulic Bendix-design self-energizing brakes that first appeared in the Ford family on Lincolns in 1939 and F-1 pickup trucks in 1947. (See chapter five.) The Bendix design became the industry standard and is still common in drum brakes today. Most important for the old Ford hot rod builder, the Bendix front brakes used on F-1 and F-100 pickups are as common as grass and bolt to old Ford axles, usually with only minor modification. And as a bonus, F-1 and F-100 pickups retained the 5 1/2-inch bolt pattern of the early Fords.

Hard steering—*"Old Ford steering was stiff and notchy, and the wheel didn't always want to return when you let go of it."*

Ford steering from the Model As through 1936 used a fixed sector that was stiff even when new, although Ford was hardly alone on this count. A simple change to a 1937 or later box with a recirculating sector (see Chapter Three) in good condition virtually eliminates steering complaints.

Finally, a common and major contributor to the old Ford myth is the fact that they were old Fords by the time they had trickled down to youthful owners. The affordable Fords were invariably well used, but not necessarily used well. Most often they received much less maintenance than they needed, and much of that was ineptly applied by the time they reached their second and third owners. Remember, these old Fords logged a good many of their miles during the Great Depression, when frequent, professional maintenance was a low priority. It's to their credit that they survived at all!

So, if the only thing that has kept you from building an old Ford hot rod is fear of the myth, put all that silliness out of your mind and get ready to have the most fun you've had since high school!

THE IMPORTANCE OF A FOCUSED PLAN
So far we've had fun talking and dreaming about building a neat, traditional roadster, and we've even worked through what may have been some lingering doubts. Now, it's time for a reality check—a look at the project in the context of the real world. As affordable as a traditional hot rod is, a good deal of time is required to carry one through from start to finish. And it just isn't going to happen without a detailed plan.

From time to time throughout your roadster project it's essential that you also submit to a focus check: Once you've developed and accepted the plan, stick with it! Even slight deviations, such as the use of a highly visible part that's way out of time with a traditional roadster, can violate the spirit of the finished car.

If you're farming out large blocks of work, be particularly vigilant for out-of-time details; few professional rod builders are building purely traditional cars today, and most are inclined to go with the bits and pieces with which they're familiar—modern street rod stuff. There's nothing wrong with street rod hardware and methods for street rods; it simply has no place on a recreation of a simple and pure postwar hot rod.

THE TIME YOU'LL NEED
On average, construction of a roadster like our Bishop-Tardel Highboy A-V8 will require 1,000 to 1,500 man-hours, excluding parts hunting. Viewed as a single block, this is a rather daunting figure, but given some perspective it's really quite reasonable. If you work on the roadster an average of 20 to 30 hours per week you will complete it in 50 weeks—just in time for a much-deserved two-week vacation on the road with your new treasure. And even if you can devote only 10 hours each week, the roadster could be ready for the road inside of two years.

If your strengths lie more in making money than building hot rods, you might be purchasing a lot of the work detailed in these pages. But whether you're doing or buying, the same amount of time is required to produce a car like the B-T Highboy.

THE SPACE YOU'LL NEED
If at all possible, dedicate an area of your garage or shop to the construction of your hot rod. Faced with those 1,000-plus hours of work, and with a real life to lead as well, you'll move the project along faster if your work environment allows you to check off some of those hours in quarter- and half-hour increments. Not every task is a big deal requiring uninterrupted hours of concentrated work, and even large tasks can be done in small pieces. But this sort of time economy won't happen if you have to set up and then knock down the project each time you work on it. Just as important, it's fun and exciting to see your hot rod grow, and a great psychological boost for those times when your energy is down and your commitment begins to flag.

The "modern" roadster style was beginning to emerge prior to World War II. In 1942 Manuel Ayulo's A-V8 lacked only a raked stance and Ford disc wheels to bring it up to postwar standards. *Bud Van Maanen*

Bill Echoff's highboy was only an axle and a set of disc wheels away from its transition to postwar style. A rail-height frame step in the rear already has that end sitting right. *Peter Eastwood*

Parts Storage

You won't need so much space that you can store all the parts for your hot rod—unless you plan to wait to begin assembly until you have everything that's needed. But you will need more space than what's required to handle just the parts for the task at hand because there will be times when you'll purchase pieces out of order, like when you happen onto a great deal on hardware you won't need for months.

Outside storage of large parts and assemblies is OK, just as long as they're protected from the weather and out of the way of people and animal traffic.

Small parts and hardware should be stored inside, organized, and labeled. Otherwise, you had better add another 100 hours to the project to cover the time you'll spend pawing through shelves and boxes, again and again, to find parts.

Workbench

We're not going to spend any time telling you how to set up your shop, because you probably already have a start on it if you're considering the project we're talking about. You do need a sturdy bench, about 2x5 feet, with a substantial vise. Some of the old parts you'll be working with must be coaxed into shape with heat and muscle.

Assembly Area

Right from the start you'll need about half a garage for your assembly area, because you'll be working with a full-size mockup of the chassis as soon as you've gathered all of the chassis pieces. Once the chassis is a roller, you can move it out into the sunshine on nice days, but watch out for encroachment in that clean, dry place inside. Agree to tarp it just for one night out-of-doors and you'll be fighting with the rest of the family to reclaim your spot. This is a given.

The Tools You Will Need

In addition to a normal complement of hand tools, you'll need a few power tools:
- Electric drill motor
- Drill press
- Small hand-held grinder to use as cutoff saw and for the hundreds of hours of grinding and metal-polishing required
- Bench- or pedestal-mounted circular sander for shaping parts, chamfering weld joints, and so on
- Bench- or pedestal-mounted belt sander for shaping and metal-polishing parts

In addition to these essential tools, you should also have access to:
- Oxyacetylene torches
- MIG wire-feed welder

From beginning to end, from mockup to completion, you'll need things to help you position parts and assemblies at different heights. These helpers include:
- Hydraulic floor jack
- At least six adjustable jackstands
- Assorted lengths of wood blocks—2x4-inch, 1x4-inch, 1/2 x4-inch, plus a dozen wooden paint-mixing sticks to use as shims
- Pairs of 4-, 6-, and 8-inch C-clamps

To make sure your roadster project is going to be fun from start to finish, protect yourself from avoidable injuries with safe work practices and good safety equipment. You will need:
- Welder's gloves—heavy leather gauntlets for handling hot parts
- Leather metal-fitter's gloves—leather palms and fingers protect your hands from sharp metal edges
- Safety glasses, safety goggles, and face shield—wear eye protection at all times
- Particle mask—3M makes a great mask that's light, comfortable, and very effective. It sells for less than $20, and the replaceable filters are about $4 a pair. Don't even think about cutting and grinding metal without a mask!

The Services You Will Need

Find a machine shop that both understands what you're doing and likes to do the work required. Thanks to the continuation of the old Ford hobby, there are good friendly services available nearly everywhere, so there's no need to put up with some reluctant sniveler who's constantly complaining about how he's losing money on your work. The local chapter of the Ford Early V-8 Club can help you find the shop you need.

Also line up body and paint services. Old sheet metal generally needs considerable work to whip it back into shape, and even new Brookville reproduction steel bodies require an expert hand to ensure correct alignment of the doors once the body is installed on the frame.

Because of the ever-changing, increasingly stringent federal, state, and local restrictions on automotive paint, the legal "driveway paint job" is a thing of the past in many areas of the country. The continuous changes in rules and regulations add up to a moving target for the paint industry, and as a result, new products are continually being introduced, making it difficult for even the painting pros to keep up. For these reasons we suggest you line up a pro with current, up-to-date experience to do your paint work. While many production body and paint shops shy away from the specialized work you require, there are lots of painters willing to moonlight, using a booth rented after normal working hours. You might also check with the vocational education department of a local high school or community college. They usually have the latest equipment and information, and many schools seek projects for their students. We also suggest you talk to a local paint dealer about sources. He'll know which shops and painters are capable of and willing to do the work you require.

Catalogs

The catalogs listed in Appendix A are important links to the folks who can provide invaluable help in building your roadster. There's overlap and redundancy of parts and products in the list, but you'll discover that each supplier has certain strengths. When one is back ordered on a needed part, you can probably find it in someone else's inventory.

Order your catalogs soon, so you'll have them by the time you're ready to start work.

Technical and Historical References

Solid old Ford technical information is plentiful and inexpensive. Most of it is either original material or reprints of Ford-produced factory manuals, parts books, and service bulletins. These books, along with several others we consider essential, are available through some of the suppliers shown in Appendix A.

The Ford Green Book

Ford's "Green Book" is one of the most valuable documents in your hot rod-building library. This 802-page treasure trove, the Ford Chassis Parts and Accessories Catalog, is packed with drawings to help you identify Ford parts. It also lets you see their relationships for assembly of such items as transmission, rear end, brakes, steering, and such. The Green Book also contains essential application information that will tell you which parts will interchange from one year to another. Best of all, the Green Book is a wonderful vehicle for getting the "feel" of old Ford parts, for getting you involved. It won't make you an overnight expert but it's a great start.

Ford Service Bulletins & Repair Manuals

If you're accustomed to the corrective Band-Aid approach of service bulletins of the last several decades, Ford's collections of detailed how-tos will seem both strange and wonderful. They are models of what service bulletins are supposed to be, with their detailed step-by-step instruction in important tasks. They made up the formal schooling for countless Ford mechanics and can provide the same expertise today for anyone in-

terested in old Ford mechanical work. In addition to concise how-to information, each service bulletin contains fit, tolerance, and wear-limit specifications that you'll find essential when servicing or rebuilding your roadster's hardware.

Don Montgomery's Hot Rod Pictorials

Don Montgomery's picture books about hot-rodding in southern California in the 1930s, 1940s, and 1950s are a great source of visual information for the type of car you are building. They're particularly valuable for ideas about details, like headlight brackets, shock absorber mounts, axle-control devices, wheels, and trim—the important little things that can either make or break the look of a hot rod.

Ron Halloran's and Ron Bishop's Flathead Books

Halloran's *Nostalgia—Rebuilding and Modifying the Flathead Ford V-8* offers great proven ideas for flat-motor hop-up. Ron Bishop's *Rebuilding the Famous Ford Flathead* is an all-around good source for working on the motor.

Tex Smith's *The Complete Ford Flathead V-8 Engine Manual*

Editor Ron Ceridono has done a wonderful job of pulling together a lot of really valuable flathead information and massaging it into a good read, as well as an essential reference book. Significantly differing opinions from some of the truly great names in flathead building emphasize the motor's flexibility.

THE PERSONAL TOUCH— MAKING IT YOUR HOT ROD

Now, a word on individualism and the personal touch: The A-V8 highboy roadster that resulted from the work in this book encompasses many proven methods utilizing old Ford hardware. Many of the engineering aspects of the car were borrowed from a generation of hot-rodders who were instrumental in the evolution of the many details that make up a successful Ford hot rod. In a sense, the roadster was built to a proven formula.

It's gratifying when an old practitioner notices and appreciates that we've handled a particular detail the way it was done correctly in the past. There's even been envy expressed on occasion, with someone wishing they'd done a certain part or alteration the way we've done it. This just illustrates that there's always room for improvement in hot-rodding, even within the tight confines of building a totally correct traditional car.

And that's what we've done with the Bishop-Tardel Highboy. Working from a 90 per-

One of our favorite As belonged to Bud Hand from the old Mojave Timing Association. Its prewar Kelseys, tall headlight stalks, just-right windshield rake, and clean frame sides contribute to the car's crisp character. *Vern Tardel collection*

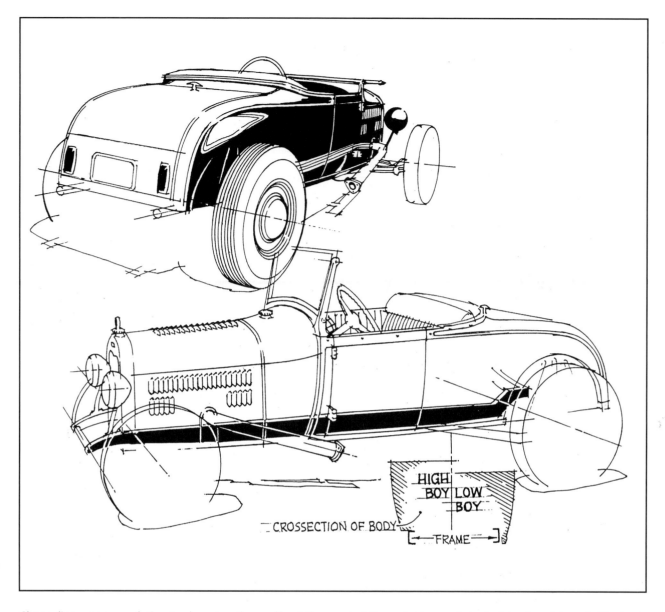

HIGH
BOY LOW
BOY

CROSSECTION OF BODY

FRAME

Channeling was one solution to dropping the profile of the car, but it required a great deal of sheet metal work. The body sides were cut loose from the floor, which usually remained in its original position atop the frame rails, while the body was dropped down over the rails and then reattached. It's little wonder that channeled cars weren't more popular, and perhaps not surprising that few of them were done really well.

cent Ford parts pile, we specified and built a hot rod that, by early 1950s standards of finish, would have been a decidedly high-end car. That, too, was a conscious part of the plan, to illustrate that there's no sin in carefully fashioned, polished, and finished parts and work in a traditional hot rod, either then or now.

There's a popular misconception that hot rods used to be either crudely finished beaters or glass-lacquered show cars. The reality lies somewhere around the middle of these extremes. The relative quality of a car was tied directly to its

owner's ability and budget; rodders strove for the best possible car their experience and money would allow, using creativity and hard work to make it special.

It was in the details that hot rods were unique and special, and it was here that owners made their cars memorable. We've only to check early editions of *Hot Rod* magazine or flip through Don Montgomery's books to see the range of cleverness in such elements as headlight mounts, nerf bars, axle control devices, exhaust systems—essential pieces that gave the early cars their individual character.

The best part is that these are the things that are still giving newly built traditional hot rods individual character today. During the construction of the Bishop-Tardel Highboy, two other 1929-bodied highboy roadsters were built in the same shop at the same time. One of them was also a 90 percenter, and the other differing only in drive-train components. In spite of work being done on all three cars by several of the same people, the roadsters are distinctly different from one another—totally personalized cars.

We tell you this to assure you that a car built following the overall plan and the important details described on these pages is very likely to be as different from the B-T car as are its two stablemates. So go for it, and build your own A-V8 highboy, creating your own detailed solutions that will make us wish we'd thought of them first. But you must promise to share the results, because that's the deal, that's the way hot-rodding works.

PUTTING IT ALL TOGETHER—SOME THOUGHTS ON BUILD AND ASSEMBLY

We've organized the work in this book as a frame-up build, just the way we put the car together. It doesn't have to be done this way; it's just that experience has shown that it's a pretty good ap-

proach with a minimum of backtracking.

Something we did that we prefer not to do was to finish the car—paint, plating, polishing and all that—before we fully assembled and drove it. We jumped ahead because of the photography required for the book, however, knowing full well that a freshly built hot rod is rarely, if ever, 100 percent from the beginning. The B-T Highboy proved to be no exception, exhibiting some teething problems that we sorted out and added to the book. Corrective work would have been a whole lot easier, however, had the car been in primer. And there were some things that we might have substantially reworked if finished paint and plated parts weren't involved. These details don't make the difference between right and wrong, but instead are just different ways of doing things that you might actually prefer. We share this suggested work where it's appropriate.

Finally, when assembling your highboy—first in unfinished shakedown form, and later painted, plated, and all sorted out—use the correct grades and amounts of lubricants at each assembly step. Don't put something together dry, counting on adding lube later. You'll forget it, and that's a promise!

The torch is now in your hands.

Jean Jones' roadster was not an A-V8; it was powered with a hot Ford straight six. We include it because of its great early stance and to demonstrate that a Model A doesn't need a Deuce grille to look good. The 1928–1929 radiator shell is just fine on the right car. We also like the whimsical "dog-bone" radiator cap.

Chapter 2

FRAME—A CLASSIC FOUNDATION

4,000,000 nearly identical frames manufactured during the four
A production, these old Ford bones are still so plentiful and inex-
to $200—you can afford to be choosy. Don't compromise. Look
frame as you can find and avoid any that show serious damage,
s to have been corrected. And stay away from a new rectangular-
ice as they are, they're strictly new street rod stuff and don't eas-
lves to the work required on a traditional hot rod.

ucky, your candidate frame will have pristine front horns, but if it
worry; new horns are available from sources such as Brookville.
osing a frame, avoid the following:

- g   • Cracking
- ch cuts   • Lots of nonoriginal holes
- g cross-members   • Excessive rust pebbling

LD BONES

egins with all those little corrections that will make your frame per-
all unnecessary brackets, such as running board arms and hood
ates, by grinding the heads off of the rivets and driving them out
ou need not remove the cowl mounting brackets that locate the
ody, although it's easier to smooth and paint the frame with these
s well as to install the body, as you'll see in chapter eight.

V-8 motor mounts, a complete '32 K-member, and a stepped rear cross-member transform a Model A frame into a real hot-rod foundation.

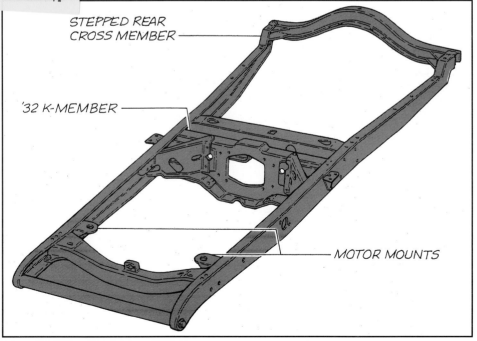

STEPPED REAR CROSS MEMBER

'32 K-MEMBER

MOTOR MOUNTS

Also, drill out the two forward hood latch holes, located just aft of the front cross-member on top of the frame, to 1/2-inch diameter. These will be used to locate the motor mounts.

Sand blast the frame inside and out to remove rust and old paint, and fill all unneeded holes with weld. You can save a great deal of finishing time by backing up the hole you're welding with a piece of copper or brass (a thick plate or the end of a length of large barstock), which won't stick to the welded steel. This ensures a flush weld on the inside of the rail and greatly reduces the time required to grind the welds flush with the surface of the frame.

Minor damage to frame horns—like wrinkling—can be corrected with some hammer-and-

1 Badly damaged frame horns are cut off square, just ahead of the front cross-member. First choice for this work is a cutoff wheel; a conventional torch leaves lots of cleanup work. A hacksaw is an okay alternative.

2 The ends of the frame rail and new horn are chamfered to ensure good weld penetration, and the two are clamped in alignment with a length of angle iron for welding.

dolly work, as can wrinkling along the frame rails. If the horns are severely damaged, replace them with new ones. Simply cut off the old ones squarely at the front of the cross-member and weld new ones in their place. Chamfer the edges along the joint before welding to ensure good penetration, and clamp the horns in alignment with the rails, using a 1- to 2-foot length of angle iron.

Finally, check the frame for squareness by measuring it diagonally, right front to left rear, then left front to right rear. The two measurements should be within 1/8 inch of one another. If they're not, have a frame pro pull it into shape before continuing on to the next steps.

MOTOR MOUNTS MADE EASY

The first frame modification is installing the motor mounts, because all the major frame work is based on the location of the engine in the frame.

There are a number of ways to make motor mounts, but we like the type shown. They're simple, they look great in a traditional roadster, and they utilize the OEM Ford motor mount hardware and pads to minimize engine vibration transmitted to the chassis. They're made from 0.125-inch-wall 2x3-inch tubing, are 4 1/2 inches long, and have a 1 1/2-inch hole drilled 1 1/2 inches from the inside end. We radiused the inside end and gave the mount some shape, although you could simply cut them off square and let it go at that, but why? So, whittle out a pair of handsome mounts and you're ready to begin the hot rod building part of this adventure.

We began by supporting the frame on stands, then positioned the motor and transmission between the rails to determine where the

3 Welded and rough blended, the new frame horn already has a fresh, crisp look—essential for this important focal point. Once the hole is drilled for the spreader bar, you'd never know it wasn't original.

motor mounts go. Since we've done all the heavy work, you can just forge ahead using the dimensions indicated.

Set the frame on stands at a comfortable working height. Clamp the mounts in place, snug against the upper surface of the frame rails, with the forward edge of the mounts 3 inches back from the center of the radiator mounting holes in the front cross-member. This position ensures sufficient clearance between the engine and the firewall at the rear of the engine, and the fan and the radiator at the front.

Check the center-to-center distance between the holes in the mounts. It should be 20 inches. If necessary, trim the ends of the mounts, where they contact the frame rails, until the distance is

correct. Keep in mind that the holes also have to be equidistant from the frame's centerline.

Tack the mounts in place with rosette welds through those forward hood-latch holes you enlarged earlier. When final welding of all the modifications and add-ons to the frame is done later, you'll stitch weld the mounts to the inside of the rails, on both sides of the mount. Done this way, you can omit a top weld and maintain the crisp line at the edge of the rail to match the one at the front cross-member, although we prefer the added assurance of welding the mount to the frame rail.

CARVING A K-MEMBER TO FIT THE A FRAME

The 1932 Ford center cross-member is the heart of a good A-V8 hot rod. Also called a K-member because of its shape, it provides the rear mount for the engine and transmission, correctly locates the brake and clutch pedals, serves as a rear mount for the front suspension wishbone, and adds a great deal of desirable stiffness that's lacking in the Model A frame. As a bonus, when the installation is done right, the K-member looks right at home, as though that was the way Henry built the frame in the first place.

With all those plusses, it stands to reason that there's some work involved in this modification. It's not hard to do; it's just a little tough to envision because it's a three-dimensional right-brain problem. The main cross-member of the K-member must be narrowed, the arms must be shortened, and they must be reduced in height for them to fit the Model A frame. The last couple of steps—shortening the arms and paring

1 Motor mounts are made from 0.125-inch wall, 2x3-inch tubing, 4 1/2 inches long. A 1 1/2-inch hole is drilled with its center 1 1/2 inches back from the outer end, for the motor mount. The radiused and shaped end gives the mount some style!

2 The finished mounts are set into the rails with their forward edge 3 inches back from the radiator mounting hole in the front cross-member. The center-to-center distance between the mounts must be 20 inches, and they must be equidistant from the frame's centerline.

3 Motor mounts must be welded to the inside of the frame, in addition to the rosette welds on the top of the rail.

down their ends—were often omitted from the installation task years ago because of the perceived difficulty involved. The result, using just the cross-member portion of the 1932 K-member, was acceptable in that it solved the hardware location and relationship problems. But the Model A ladder frame was scarcely improved, and particularly so since the original Model A center cross-member was usually removed "to save weight." The legs were also often omitted to accommodate a 1939 pedal assembly, which simplified the upgrade to hydraulic brakes. In fact, it's not uncommon to find old '32 hot rods in which the left leg has been removed or shortened when a 1939 pedal assembly was installed.

The job of adapting the complete K-member, while not all that hard, nonetheless was lavished on only a small percentage of the A-V8s built, so what you're about to do to your car is guaranteed to make it very special—one of the best.

To give you courage for tackling the job, we've provided detailed dimensioned drawings. Nonetheless, you'll have to exercise your head as you do the work, comparing your real-world parts to our measurements. Remember, folks—this is hot-roddin'. And remember, too, that you're going to do it like the very best of the old-time rodders.

To fit the 1932 K-member to the Model A frame, you must first take the K-member apart by grinding the heads off of the rivets and knocking them out.

Next, bolt the transmission case to the engine block and set them in place, with complete motor-mount pads in front, and the transmission supported with a jack. Place a straight edge across the frame just behind the transmission mount and mark the locations for the front edge of the 1932 cross-member. This should be 5 3/4 inches ahead of the front surface of the existing Model A center cross-member. Then, measure the distance between the inside surface of the rails at the mark. This distance should be about 29 3/4 inches. Divide the distance by two—14 7/8 inches. Find and mark the center of the 1932 cross-member, then make a mark on each end, 14 7/8 inches from the center mark.

Mark and trim the cross-member, referring to the drawing on page 29. Use a cutting torch, plasma cutter, or cutoff wheel for the work.

Install the trimmed 1932 cross-member in the frame and bolt it to the transmission mount. The forward edge of the cross-member should line up with the marks you made on the frame earlier. Now, clamp the cross-member in place. Then, drill two holes in each rail and down through the cross-member, and bolt the cross-member to the frame.

Next, heat the ends of the cross-member floor evenly along a line perpendicular to the face of the cross-member, and bend the ends up into contact with the frame. The easiest way to do this is have an assistant progressively tighten a couple of large C-clamps to draw the metal into position as it's heated.

When the cross-member floor is positioned against the bottom of the frame rails, let it cool with the clamps in place. Then, drill three 3/8-inch holes through the cross-member and the frame and bolt the pieces together with Grade 8 bolts. Then, remove the C-clamps. Later, during final welding of the frame, you'll "stitch" the new seams together.

Next, section and trim the K-member legs with a torch, plasma cutter, or cutoff wheel, weld the ends to the shortened legs, and add the little fillet pieces. Finally, grind and shape the welds and bolt the shortened legs in place with Grade 8 bolts to complete what looks for all the world like a factory-made K-member—Model A style!

Now, one final note on the K-member modification: If you can't locate an original 1932 K-member, or haven't the tools and skills to modify one, Vern Tardel offers a reproduction K-member that's sized to fit a stock Model A frame and does all the things the stock one does. (See Appendix A.)

THE RIGHT STEP FOR THE REAR CROSS-MEMBER

To achieve the all-important correct stance of a just-right A-V8 highboy roadster, the rear of the chassis must be dropped 5 to 6 inches from its stock height. By recontouring the rear spring, reversing the eyes, and eliminating some unnecessary leaves, you can drop the rear 2 or 3 inches (see Chapter Four). "Stepping" the rear cross-member will account for an additional 3 inches. Stepping, also called "Z'ing," simply means that the rear of the frame is cut off a few inches forward of the cross-member, moved up, and rewelded, creating a step in the frame. The net effect is that the spring pocket in the rear cross-member is raised several inches, which lowers the frame and thus the rear of the car.

Stepping the frame also requires some body modifications because the relocated rear cross-member will intrude into the body floor. The work isn't difficult, as you'll see in chapter eight, and the effort is paid back with a great look!

Mark the frame rails 4 inches from the forward face of the rear cross-member. This isn't an arbitrary dimension; if the cut for the step is made 1/4 or 1/2 inch farther forward, lots of otherwise unnecessary bodywork will be required. Use a square to mark the vertical cuts, and care-

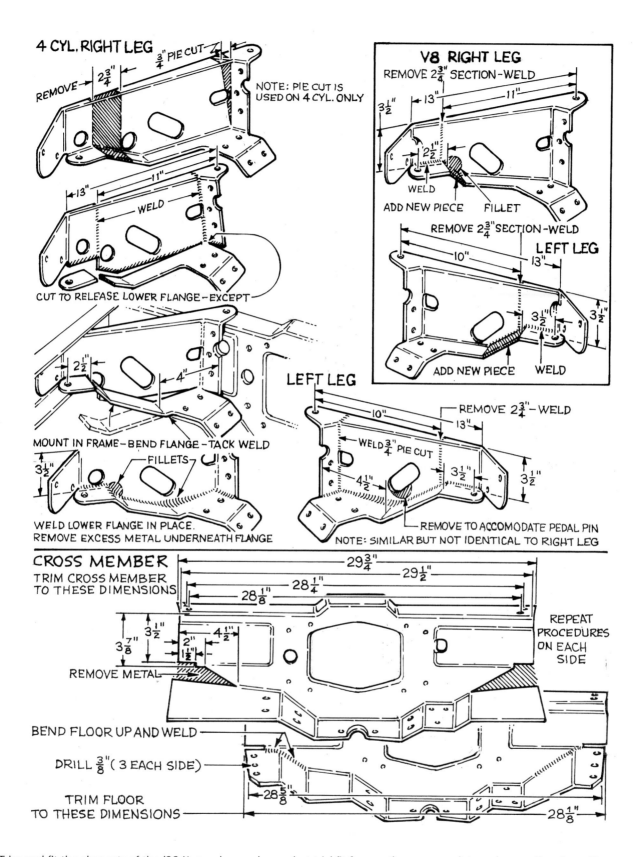

4 CYL. RIGHT LEG

¾" PIE CUT

REMOVE 2¾"

NOTE: PIE CUT IS USED ON 4 CYL. ONLY

13"　11"

WELD

CUT TO RELEASE LOWER FLANGE – EXCEPT

2½"　4"

MOUNT IN FRAME – BEND FLANGE – TACK WELD

FILLETS

3½"

WELD LOWER FLANGE IN PLACE. REMOVE EXCESS METAL UNDERNEATH FLANGE

V8 RIGHT LEG

REMOVE 2¾" SECTION – WELD

3½"　13"　11"

2½"

WELD

ADD NEW PIECE　FILLET

REMOVE 2¾" SECTION – WELD

LEFT LEG

10"　13"

3½"

3½"

ADD NEW PIECE　WELD

LEFT LEG

10"

REMOVE 2¾" – WELD

13"

WELD ¾" PIE CUT

4½"　3½"　3½"

REMOVE TO ACCOMODATE PEDAL PIN

NOTE: SIMILAR BUT NOT IDENTICAL TO RIGHT LEG

CROSS MEMBER

TRIM CROSS MEMBER TO THESE DIMENSIONS

29¾"

29½"

28¼"

28⅛"

3½"　4½"

3⅞"　2"

1½"

REMOVE METAL

REPEAT PROCEDURES ON EACH SIDE

BEND FLOOR UP AND WELD

DRILL ⅜" (3 EACH SIDE)

TRIM FLOOR TO THESE DIMENSIONS

28⅝"

28⅛"

Trim and fit the elements of the '32 K-member as shown, but trial fit frequently as you work to make sure the pieces fit your frame before you do any final welding.

1 Location for the front edge of the 1932 cross-member is marked 5 3/4 inches ahead of the front of the existing Model A cross-member.

2 The trim dimensions from the drawing on page 22 are transferred to the cross-member.

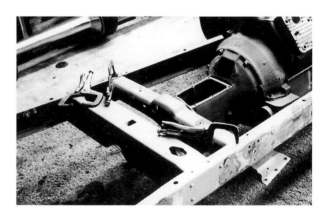

3 The cross-member is trimmed to its new shape. If a conventional torch is used, trimming should be slightly oversize and then finished with a grinder. Unless you're really good with a torch, we recommend a cutoff wheel for this work.

4 The transmission mount is bolted to the cross-member and the transmission, and is clamped in the frame. Then, two holes are drilled through the frame rail and the cross-member so the cross-member can be bolted to the frame rails.

fully cut the rear section off of the frame, keeping all the cuts square.

Move the rear frame section up, lining up the bottom of the rear section with the top of the forward section. Square and clamp the two sections, and tack them together, taking care to maintain the alignment.

Cut and fit fillets, made from 2x4-inch 1/8-inch channel, to the new frame junctions. Tack the fillets in place, checking the alignment of the frame sections as you work. This is a relatively critical situation, in that you don't want the heat from welding to wrack the frame and pull it out of shape. While the ideal situation would be to do this work on a frame jig or table, the job can be handled neatly with patient and constant checking of the alignment of the two sections as the welding is done progressively from side to side.

Finally, trim the ends of the rear cross-member flush with the outer surface of the frame. This allows the cross-member to fit up inside the body once the body modifications are done.

It would seem to be a good idea to box the frame step with a plate on the inside of each rail just to make sure the new joints are strong enough, but we're not so sure that that's so.

5 A line, drawn on the "floor" of the cross-member, perpendicular to its front edge, locates the point where the floor will be bent up to meet the lower edge of the frame.

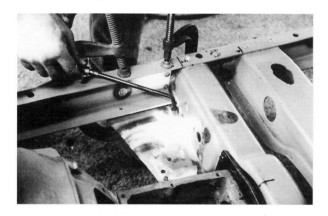

6 The floor is heated along the line as an assistant tightens large C-clamps to draw the end of the floor up and into contact with the lower edge of the frame rail. The cross-member is then allowed to cool before it's drilled and bolted to the frame.

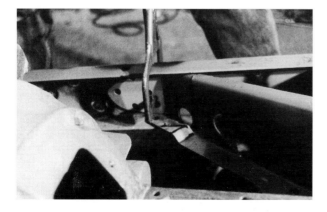

7 The large portion of the shortened leg is bolted to the cross-member, the trimmed end is fitted to the frame rail, and the two pieces are tacked together.

8 This comparison of the original left leg and the shortened right side shows the amount of whittling required to fit the legs to the Model A frame.

9 All pared down, stitched back together, and with the welds blended, the Deuce K-member looks right at home in the Model A frame.

Here's why: While the addition of the 1932 K-member adds some torsional resistance to the total frame, it doesn't make the frame rigid, even in the area where it's installed. There's still some flexibility, and that flexibility increases as forces move outward from the K-member. This is OK, because we're not trying to transform the frame into a torsionally rigid structure; we just want to improve it within reasonable limits that were known and available in the postwar cars—and within the abilities of the old frames to accept improvements.

We don't want to suddenly arrest that natural, radiating flexibility in an early chassis, and that's just what boxing plates on the rear cross-member step would do. The effect would be to concentrate forces at the forward edges of the boxing plates, which could cause fractures in the frame rails at these points. So, unless the entire frame is carefully and continuously boxed, the rear cross-member step shouldn't be boxed.

THE 1932 FRAME—MORE GREAT BONES

The Deuce frame was a popular platform for Model A roadster bodies in the 1930s, 1940s, and 1950s, and while the combination was not an A-V8 in the strictest sense, the appellation has been used so often for the Model A/Deuce hybrid that it's generally accepted.

As with a Model A-framed A-V8, modern fabricated boxed Deuce rails just don't look right in an early-style car. Original 1932 frames, in good condition, are pricey and usually considerably less than perfect, sporting old collision damage, badly rusted surfaces, and lots more holes than Henry punched in them.

As an alternative to a time-consuming search for a good set of 1932 bones, you can build a fresh Deuce frame using a pair of new rails from American Stamping Company or Speedway Motors, plus an original 1932 K-member, and original Model A front and rear cross-members. The new rails are stamped from 10-gauge steel and include only body-mounting holes and holes for the front and rear spreader bars. Otherwise, they are perfect and unblemished. The nicest part about this approach—other than a low price of $525 for the rails—is they need no repairs. There are no bends to straighten, no cracks or unwanted holes to weld, and no rust!

An excellent 1932 K-member will fetch $100–$300, and good Model A front and rear cross-members are about $25–$50 apiece, setting the cost of a new frame at $675–$775. With repairable original frames selling for $750 and more, the new frame is a deal. If you can't locate a stock K-member, contact Vern Tardel. He offers a reproduction K-member that is dimension-

1 The cut for stepping the rear of the frame is made 4 inches from the face of the rear cross-member. It's important to make the cut clean and square with the frame rail.

2 The cross-member and fillets are chamfered and then welded on both the inside and outside of the joint.

3 The welds on the outside surfaces are ground and blended, and the ends of the cross-member are trimmed flush with the outer face of the frame for clearance with the body.

ally and functionally identical to the original. (See Appendix A.)

The dimensions shown in the illustration on page 2-24 ensure that the cowl, at the firewall, is even with the sides of the rails, and the body

THE FORD REAR AXLE—
A RACE TRACK VETERAN

The Ford "banjo" differential was a staple in circle track, dry lakes, and drag racing not so many years ago. With a standard—and most common—4.11:1 gear ratio, the banjo was made to order for the quarter mile, whether it ran straight ahead on asphalt or bent into an oval on dirt. And when you added a quick-change center section, you had a race car differential that was as good as they got, whose basic layout lives on today in live-axle setups from Winters, Frankland, and venerable old Halibrand.

1 A 3/4-inch section is removed from the right-side 1947–1948 passenger car lower rear shock mount to make it the same length as the left-side shock mount.

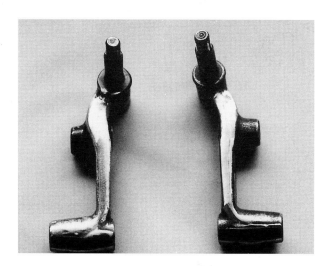

2 Welded and blended, the right-side shock mount is now a mirror image of the left one.

The Full Ford Axle, Banjo and All

The Ford banjo rear end works just fine most of the time. Nonetheless, sheared axle keys and even broken axle ends are not uncommon when the driveline is hammered with a lot of horsepower—or abusive silliness. While a sheared axle key is little more than an annoyance, a broken axle can have serious consequences when the newly released rear wheel, hub, and axle end part company with the car. We'll show you how to prevent such embarrassment later on in this section.

The 1935–1941 Ford rear end is the traditional mainstay for A-V8 hot rods because it provided much-needed strength for lively flatheads and is just the right size. Even the Deuce third member, possibly an improvement over the Model A version—although there's little evidence to support this notion—was routinely changed out for a later unit.

The basic differential unit changed little throughout its production life. The banjo housing is the same from 1935 through 1948, even carrying the same Ford part number. There are a few internal differences, the most important being the spiders, with differentials made up into 1938 sharing the 12-tooth gears (Part No. 18-4215) with all units back to 1932, while some 1938s and 1939 and later units had 11-tooth spiders (Part No. 81A-4215).

Gear ratios were either 4.11:1 (Part No. 48-4209D Set) or 3.78:1 (Part No. 68-4209A Set). Axle length from 1935 to 1941 was 32.85 inches per side—about 3/4 inch longer than the 1932—and 33.70 inches from 1942 through 1948. The 1942–1948 version can be used for a highboy A-V8, but some extra backspace is needed on the rear wheels to keep them close to the body.

(NOTE: These are Ford part numbers that are still used by most suppliers of old Ford parts.)

While it's possible to piece together a Ford rear end, it can be a long search to match up all the related parts. The very best approach is to find a complete, sound, working rear end assembly to start with. It's much easier.

The Halibrand Quick-Change—
Vintage High Tech

The Halibrand quick-change rear end has long been one of hot-rodding's hot buttons—a gotta-have piece of hardware that was trick and just expensive enough to put it out of the reach of most rodders. The price situation hasn't changed much over the years; it's still kind of pricey, particularly when purchased new. Yes, new. Old-style Halibrand V-8 quick-change hardware from bare center-section castings to complete turnkey rear ends and everything along the way are available directly from Halibrand (see Appendix A). If you're a

The Ford banjo is hot-rod right and still looks pretty good under the rear of a highboy roadster. Plentiful and inexpensive, it's strong enough for moderately hopped-up flatheads as long as it's not abused.

real worrywart, Halibrand can build a unit for you, using your Ford axle bells, with Ford 9-inch-style retained axles and bearings. This setup will handle three times the horsepower you're likely to coax from your streetable flatmotor.

Halibrand also has some interesting variants worth considering, like the "no-change" banjo, which is simply an aluminum Ford style center section. These are no longer made but they do show up at swap meets. Then, if you love everything about a quick-change except the ever-present gear whine, there are helical-cut gears available in place of the straight-cut howlers. And if you like the Halibrand look but have a tight budget and don't really care about the quick-change capability, Halibrand now makes a case that looks like a quick change but uses stock Ford differential components. The change-gear case is 2 inches shorter than the regular case—so it will fit under a stock Deuce without hitting the gas tank—but otherwise looks like the real article. Officially, this piece is

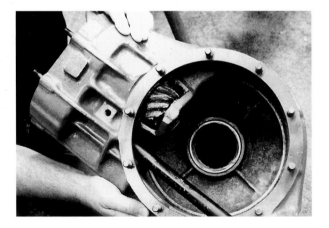

The pinion bearing cage in this old magnesium case cracked when the cage cooled—not uncommon for early cases where machining was less than precise. The real problem is that this is a front drive case—three speeds in reverse!

The ultimate hot-rod rear-end—the Halibrand V-8 quick-change. Available either brand new or as a swap-meet treasure, it's still one of the trickest pieces you can add to your highboy.

no longer in production, but Halibrand has a few left in stock at this writing.

There is also a fair supply of old Halibrands on the swap meet circuit, and you might want to pay particular attention to events featuring old race cars. A lot of veteran QCs have led tough lives and show it, but there are a lot of serviceable

The helical change gears on the left are virtually silent when compared to the more traditional straight-cut howlers. The helical gears require special thrust bearings in the end cover and one in the change case.

ones to be had for much less money than you'd spend for a new one.

There are three basic units to consider—the Model A type, perfectly fine for a street-driven A-V8; the V-8 type, absolutely on target and capable of handling some serious flathead horsepower; and the Champ car style, a little large for an A-V8 but a wicked-looking bit of hardware that has serious written all over it. Most center sections are cast aluminum, although rare magnesium versions show up now and then.

External scars and scuffs are of little concern, but watch out for evidence of lots of repairs, like welds on top of welds and heavy galling of the webs. A great many of these old warriors have spent their lives beneath dirt track cars, getting "backed into the wall a time or two" as the old guys are fond of pointing out. There's something special about having an old original piece under the rear of your roadster, but there's also a lot to be said for a strong, true, brand-new case. At a little more than $400 for a fresh V-8 case, it doesn't make a lot of sense to struggle with an old one that needs lots of work.

As a final caution about buying a case from a private party, make certain the left side of the

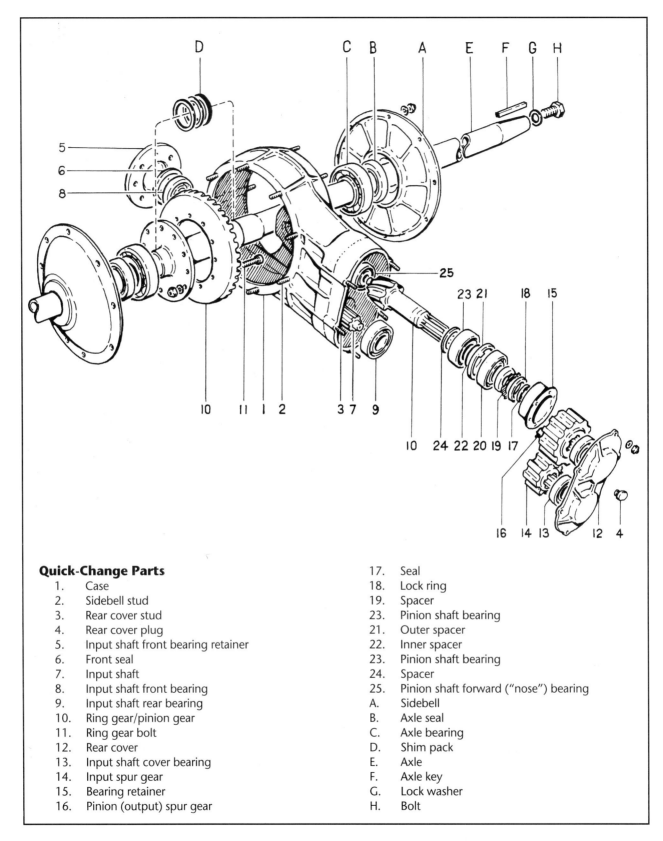

Quick-Change Parts

1. Case
2. Sidebell stud
3. Rear cover stud
4. Rear cover plug
5. Input shaft front bearing retainer
6. Front seal
7. Input shaft
8. Input shaft front bearing
9. Input shaft rear bearing
10. Ring gear/pinion gear
11. Ring gear bolt
12. Rear cover
13. Input shaft cover bearing
14. Input spur gear
15. Bearing retainer
16. Pinion (output) spur gear
17. Seal
18. Lock ring
19. Spacer
23. Pinion shaft bearing
21. Outer spacer
22. Inner spacer
23. Pinion shaft bearing
24. Spacer
25. Pinion shaft forward ("nose") bearing
A. Sidebell
B. Axle seal
C. Axle bearing
D. Shim pack
E. Axle
F. Axle key
G. Lock washer
H. Bolt

Essentially unchanged since Ted Halibrand designed it in the late 1940s, the Halibrand quick-change is still viable today, thanks to the availability of each and every part—brand new!

pinion-support web is the open side, with clearance for the ring gear. There were QC center sections built for front-axle drive, such as you would use on a four-wheel-drive Bonneville car. Unless you're assembling Halibrand quick-changes on a regular basis, it's likely you wouldn't even notice.

The Halibrand can be a little tricky to assemble, so you might consider entrusting the work to someone who does it as a regular thing, like roundy-round race car shops or even a hard-core oval track racer who does his own work. If you feel up to the task, just pay attention to the big diagram (page 44), get the case uniformly hot before pressing in any bearings, and resist the temptation to pick up a hammer or mallet; when everything's OK gentle force works best.

Making Rear-Wheel Bearing Races Good As New

Worn wheel bearing races on old Ford axle housings may seem like a hopeless situation, but they're actually a common malady that's easily corrected, thanks to replacement sleeve-type races available through many of the old Ford parts sources. You'll also need the services of one of those old-Ford-friendly machine shops we talked about earlier, unless you have a very large lathe with at least a 14-inch swing and a 30-inch bed, plus a big rosebud torch to soften the old races. And, of course, you'll need a tall press to install the new bearing races. That Ford-friendly machine shop is looking better and better all the time, isn't it?

We had the races on the roadster's 1940 rear end renewed by Craft Engine Machine in Santa Rosa, California, for $70. The new sleeves were purchased at All Ford Parts in Campbell, California, for $55. Few modern automotive machine shops have lathes large enough for this job, so you might try one specializing in large truck or farm machinery work. They will probably have a crankshaft grinder large enough to remove the races that way rather than with a lathe.

If a lathe is used for the work, the ends of the housings must be thoroughly heated and allowed to cool slowly to take the hardness out of the old races before cutting them down to accept the new races. The new races should require only moderate pressure to press them onto the housing.

Safety Hubs—Someone Else's Better Idea

Long ago, race-sanctioning organizations decreed the use of some form of wheel retention in the event of axle breakage. A number of schemes were used, including one of the more successful ones that has survived and is available today. Called a safety hub, the device consists of a two-piece retainer; one piece bolts to the axle housing and the other piece is welded to the wheel hub. Safety hubs regularly show up at swap meets and new ones are available from sources like Speedway Motors at about $50 a set, or from Vern Tardel for $30 (see Appendix A). That's really pretty cheap insurance, and they're just as important for a street-driven Ford hot rod as they are on race cars.

Speedway Safety Hubs

The safety hub retainer block, which bolts to the axle housing, has a raised land around the hole for the wheel hub. The ID of the land is smaller than the OD of the retainer ring, which is welded to the hub. Thus, the hub is trapped in the retainer block and can't separate from the axle housing until the retainer block is unbolted.

The hole in the safety hub retainer, which bolts to the brake backing plate, is smaller than the ring, which is spot welded to the wheel hub inside the drum. This prevents the drum from moving outward more than a fraction of an inch should the axle break.

Ford rear-wheel bearing races are renewed with new sleeves pressed onto the ends of the axle housings after the worn or damaged hardened surface has been turned down.

The Halibrand dummy case uses either a Ford or Halibrand ring and pinion set with a front-mounted pinion just like stock, hence no quill shaft, change gears, or noise. Sadly, Halibrand is no longer producing this wonderful piece.

The Tardel drum retainer bolts onto the rear of Ford backing plates, using two of the wheel cylinder mounting holes. It's simple and effective, permitting the drum to move outward no more than 1/8 inch.

Safety hubs are easy to install, but the opening in the retainer in new ones may have to be enlarged, either on a lathe or with a die grinder, to clear the wheel hub. It's no big deal if you know about it beforehand. And, of course, there's a little welding involved, with a wire-feed or arc welder rather than a gas torch.

First check the fit of the retainer block on the housing to make sure it clears the shoulder on the housing that aligns the brake backing plate. The retainer block must also fit flush against the plate. Then, check the fit of the retainer block on the hub to make sure it's at least flush with the end of the hub. If necessary, increase the ID of the retainer until it is. Otherwise, the hub will bind in the retainer when it's installed. Install the backing plate on the axle housing with two of the original bolts, located diagonally opposite of one another.

Coat the threads of the retainer block studs with Loctite, and screw them into the block. Check the fit of the block to the axle housing. It should slide easily into position. If it doesn't, align the mounting holes through the backing plate, axle housing, and radius rods with a 1/2-inch drill.

Fit the retainer block over the hub and set the retainer ring in position, flush with the end of the hub, in preparation to welding. Stuff a damp rag into the hub to absorb some of the welding heat. Tack the retainer ring to the hub to hold it in place, and weld it at four locations, 90 degrees apart, with 1/2- to 3/4-inch longweld beads.

Use new axle keys when you put the rear end back together (unless the old ones are perfect), and make sure the taper on the key is at the inside, facing down. When you install the hubs, feed the safety hub studs through the holes in the backing plates and axle housing and hold the safety hub in place with split washers and regular nuts. Finally, screw on and torque the axle nuts to 140–160 foot-pound and lock them in place with fresh cotter pins.

Tardel's Brake Drum Retainers

Vern Tardel's safety device for 1939–1948 passenger car brakes is a simple clamp that prevents the drum from parting from the brake. I made similar clamps for the rear drums on my first roadster in the 1950s, but my design required removing the drums to install the clamps. OK, they were a little complicated, but I was only 15 years old at the time, so give me a break!

Vern's retainers simply bolt to the backing plate using two of the wheel cylinder bolt holes and fit over the drum flange to keep the drum from moving away from the hub should an axle break. It couldn't be simpler. But, then, Vern is a lot older than 15.

DRIVELINE—MORE RIGHT STUFF FROM THE FAMILY PARTS PILE

The driveshaft in the Ford torque-tube driveline changed several times in the 1930s. The solid 1932 shaft fits only the 1932 rear end and is a noncontender. The 1937 shaft, which lasted through 1948, is solid and is supported at midlength with a bearing in the torque tube to prevent the shaft from whipping. This arrangement makes it a difficult shaft to shorten to fit the A-V8. The 1935–1936 shaft is a double-taper tubular shaft needing no midlength support, but it's difficult to shorten because of its design.

The constant-diameter tubular 1933–1934 shaft is ideal for shortening because it needs no midlength support and can be shortened at the rear. You'll need a 10-to-6-spline adapter (Part No. 48-4684—check your old Ford parts catalogs) that has been turned down on the 10-spline end to fit inside the shaft. The spline adapter is necessary because the 1937–1948 pinion has 6 splines (the 1933–1934 has 10), and while the splines of the 10-spline end are not used, the larger end of the adapter provides the added diameter that's needed to fit inside the driveshaft tube.

Now, it would be wonderful if we could tell you, with 100 percent assurance, that if you used all the dimensions listed in Chapter Two to locate the motor mounts, the K-member, and the rear cross-member you could simply shorten the driveshaft to X-number of inches and be done. That's too risky.

Instead, we recommend that you first shorten the torque tube to fit between the transmission U-joint, with the polished slide bell in place, and the flange on the rear end. Note the original length of the torque tube—61 7/8 inches for a 1933–1934 tube—beforehand, and then subtract the shortened length.

Now, measure the driveshaft and subtract the difference between the original and shortened length of the torque tube to determine the final length of the driveshaft. Do this, and if the torque tube fits, so will the driveshaft!

Shortening the driveshaft is a job for a professional driveline service with the equipment and experience to ensure that the finished shaft is true, strong, and the correct length. Plan on spending $75–$125, depending on where you live. You'll have to supply the shaft and the spline adapter and tell them how long you want the finished shaft to be.

The radius-rod lug on the torque tube will have to be repositioned to mate with the radius rods. You'll have to shorten 1933–1934 radius rods about 14 inches and heat and bend them inward at the axle housing. Radius rods from 1946 to 1948 Fords need only a slight heat-assisted

The 10-spline end of a 10-to-6 spline adapter is turned down to fit inside the trimmed 1933–1934 driveshaft, then welded all the way around.

The opening in the rear end of the shortened 1933–1934 torque tube is enlarged about 1/16 inch with a die grinder so the tube will fit over the larger 1937–1948 pinion bearing.

A 1/4-inch hole is drilled through the sleeve and pinion shaft, and a Grade 8 bolt and Nyloc nut are installed.

Before the driveshaft and torque tube are connected to the transmission, the front U-joint must be given a generous filling with Lubriplate or an equivalent grease. It's futile to attempt to correctly lube this joint through the Zerk fitting in the housing.

In addition to a new gasket on the mounting flange, apply a bead of RTV sealer to the polished ball cover before installing it.

bend at the backing plate. Just make sure the lug is positioned at least a couple of inches from the front shaft bearing that's located inside the torque tube so the bearing won't be damaged during welding.

The opening in the rear end of the 1933–1934 torque tube must be enlarged slightly to fit over the larger pinion bearing outer race, which protrudes from the banjo about 1/4 inch.

The difference in diameter is only about 1/16 inch, so the work can be done easily with a die grinder.

Finally, don't despair if you can't find a 1933–1934 driveshaft and torque tube. That pro driveline service can make a fresh driveshaft from heavy-wall (0.120 inch) 2-inch tubing and the ends from a 1937–1948 driveshaft. You can also use the later torque tube. Just knock out the center bearing after it's shortened.

Chapter 5

BRAKES, WHEELS, AND TIRES

WHEN HENRY GAVE US A BRAKE

Ford hydraulic brakes manufactured from 1939 to 1948 were popular for post-war Ford hot rods because they were readily available, fit without fuss, and worked so much better than the mechanical, random wheel-lockers that, up to that point, Henry thought were good enough. The remembered positive performance of Ford's first hydraulic brake design fades—please excuse the pun—in light of the Bendix-style brakes that became the standard in the late 1940s.

Ford vs. Bendix—A Matter of Dollars and Cents

The big difference between Ford and Bendix brakes is that the early Ford hydraulic brake is a fixed shoe-pivot design in which hydraulic pressure alone moves the shoes out and into contact with the drum. With this design, increased braking action requires increased hydraulic pressure, which requires increased pedal pressure. In short, the more braking you need, the harder you have to stand on the pedal. It sounds like a fair trade-off until we look at an even better idea—the Bendix brake.

Whether based on Ford-design brakes or the self-energizing Bendix stoppers found on Lincolns and postwar Ford pickups, "juice" brakes are an essential—and bolt-on—upgrade. Picking the right wheels and tires is just plain fun!

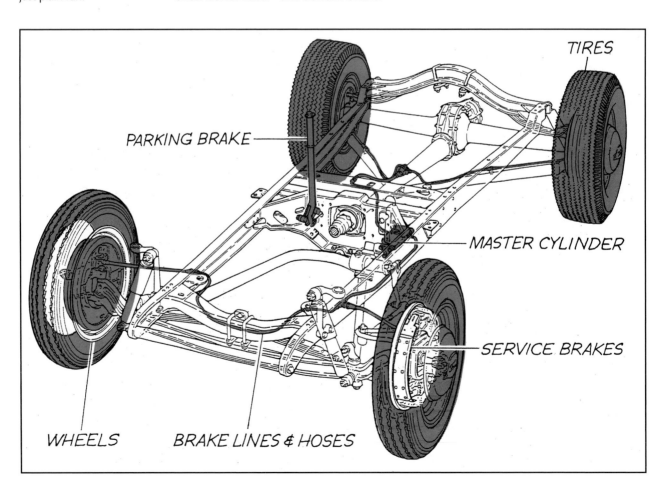

PARKING BRAKE

TIRES

MASTER CYLINDER

SERVICE BRAKES

WHEELS

BRAKE LINES & HOSES

Henry's juice brake. The wheel cylinder mounts at the very top of the backing plate, and the fixed shoe pivots can be seen at the bottom.

The Bendix brake, like this big Lincoln unit, has a large anchor pin at the top of the backing plate, above the wheel cylinder, and no fixed pivots at the bottom.

The Bendix is a self-energizing brake in which the shoes—also driven by hydraulic pressure—not only move outward to contact the drum, but the smaller primary shoe pushes the bottom of the secondary shoe against the drum, adding mechanical force to the hydraulic force to increase braking action.

Now here's some more good news. You don't have to abandon the all-Ford parts concept for your hot rod to have Bendix brakes, because they were used on some Ford products as early as 1939. In fact, some of the best old "Ford" brakes are the 1939–1948 Lincoln-Zephyr brakes, which are Bendix self-energizing units. They're harder to find than Ford passenger car brakes, but it's worth the search, because they work so well and were the hot setup in the 1940s and 1950s. The early Lincoln brakes, 1939–1940, fit on 1937–1946 Ford spindles, but the 1941–1948 brakes, with wider drums and deepset backing plates, require Lincoln spindles or modified 1947–1948 Ford spindles. The kingpin inclination of Lincoln spindles is different from that of Ford spindles. Ford spindles are 2–3 degrees positive, on a Ford axle, while Lincoln spindles are about 1 degree negative on the same axle, requiring some adjustment of the beam.

And here's even more news; the brakes used on 1948 and later Ford F-1/F-100 pickups were also Bendix self-energizing units. They're plentiful, affordable, and just as good as rare Lincoln brakes. Plus, the truck brakes fit Ford passenger-car spindles with only a slight bit of whittling required at the top of the spindle flange to clear the wheel cylinder. The rears won't fit without substantial modification of the backing plates, however, but the Ford rear brakes and Bendix fronts work well together.

Finally, there's nothing wrong with Ford fixed-pivot brakes. They are a direct bolt-on installation for 1937–1948 Ford spindles and are easily adapted to 1932–1936 spindles with a simple four-piece kit available from most of the old-Ford parts sources. The Ford brakes, however, will require more frequent adjustment than Bendix brakes.

**Putting on the Brakes—
Some Installation Guidelines**
When it comes to brakes, be good to yourself, and to anyone else who may ride with you, and start with all-new or rebuilt major components and new or reconditioned incidental hardware.

Riveted brake lining is available for old Ford and Bendix shoes. Just make sure the shoes are sound with no cracks or damage to the webs or platforms. And, when you have a good set, clean and protect them with a light coat of paint to keep them from rusting.

Unless you're an experienced brake person, purchase new wheel cylinders or have the old ones professionally rebuilt. It's not fun, glamorous work—not like porting a block—and it's

Spindles are buried deep in the big postwar Lincoln brake, requiring the use of Lincoln spindles. But gawd, do they stop!

The Bendix front brake is virtually unchanged, no matter if it's from an old Lincoln from the 1940s or a Ford truck from the 1950s. Note the position of the adjuster, and that the primary shoe is at the front on this 1948 Ford example.

not worth dealing with potential problems that can arise from less-than-perfect first-time efforts. Keep it fun and safe.

You can do some essential reconditioning work with the mechanical hardware—springs, levers, adjusters—and get the feel of the job in the process. Start by thoroughly cleaning the hardware and replacing any springs that are badly rusted; if they're just dirty, they can be cleaned, painted, and reused. Don't bother saving the shoe hold-down rods and cups because they cost only about two bucks a wheel brand new. And give yourself a future break by repainting springs in their original coded colors. This will eliminate confusion when they may have to be replaced later on.

Put your brakes back together just as they came apart. Add a wipe of high-temp lube to the flats on the backing plates where the shoes ride, to the upper shoe pivots where they contact the large post at the top of the backing plate, and to the ends of the shoe pushrods that slip into the rubber cups on the wheel cylinders.

On Bendix brakes, install the shoes with the primary shoe—the one with the shorter lining—at the front. On Ford fixed-anchor brakes the short shoe goes to the rear. Run the adjusters all the way in, with antiseize lube on the threads, and align the adjuster wheel with the adjusting slot in the backing plate.

Later, when the drums and wheels are in-

This 50-year-old Lincoln rear brake is little different from Bendix brakes in wide use today. All that dates it is the absence of an automatic adjuster. All of the hardware on this unit can be found on the bubble-pack racks of any auto parts store.

stalled, adjust the brakes by extending the adjusters until the shoes just begin to make contact with the drum and you can still turn the wheel by hand.

On Ford brakes with adjustable bottom anchors, begin by adjusting the top end of the shoes to move them into light contact with the drum. Next, with an assistant applying light pedal pressure, adjust the bottom anchors until the shoes lightly contact the drum, then tighten the lock nuts.

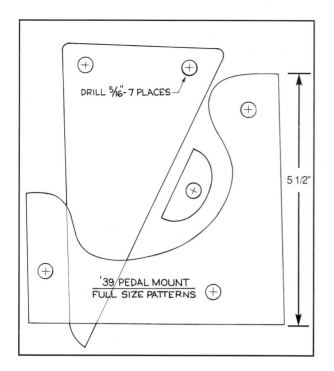

DRILL 5/16" - 7 PLACES

5 1/2"

'39 PEDAL MOUNT
FULL SIZE PATTERNS

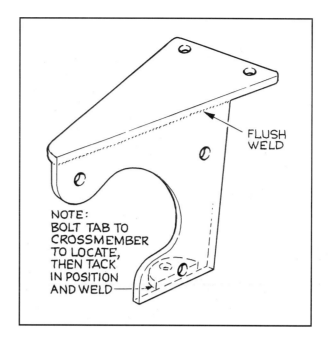

FLUSH WELD

NOTE:
BOLT TAB TO
CROSSMEMBER
TO LOCATE,
THEN TACK
IN POSITION
AND WELD

This simple mount, made of 1/4-inch steel plate, attaches a 1939 pedal/master-cylinder assembly to a '32 cross-member. It can be used with or without the left K-member leg. Photocopy the image, enlarge it to the 5 1/2-inch dimension shown, and use it for a pattern.

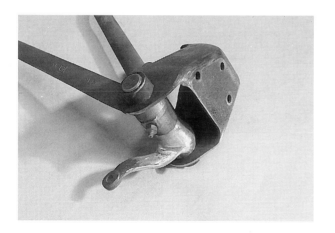

Converting a 1932 Ford pedal assembly from mechanical to hydraulic brakes involves moving the brake arm to the bottom of the sleeve. With a smooth blend of a high-quality, built-up weld on a deep chamfer, the arm is strong and safe.

You can also use a 1939 Ford pedal assembly. The bracket to hold a 1939 pedal/master cylinder mount bolts to the 1932 cross-member. When the master cylinder is installed, the cross-member is sandwiched between the mount and the cylinder base.

Pedals—Almost Made to Order

The 1939 pedal assembly was popular for A-V8s and even Deuces in the 1940s and 1950s, because it provided a master cylinder mount and connection to the brake pedal in one neat package. But it had its own problems in that the pedals had to be modified to fit the earlier bodies and frames. More important, the left leg of the 1932 K-member had to be removed or at least whittled

This master cylinder bracket, designed for the 1932 pedal assembly and made from 1/4-inch steel plate, bolts directly to the Deuce K-member, using existing holes.

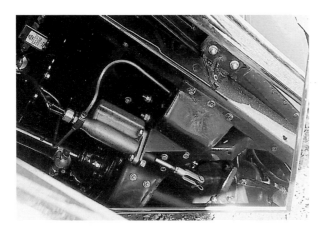

The mount locates the master cylinder on the back of the 1932 Ford cross-member. It can be filled from above through a hole in the floorboard, or as we do—with a small plunger-type oil can.

down until it was no longer of much use as a structural element. Nonetheless, we've included a pattern for the pedal bracket just in case you have your heart set on using 1939 pedals.

We prefer the 1932 pedal assembly because it bolts right onto the K-member, of course, and requires only relocation of the brake rod arm and fabrication of a simple flat bracket for the master cylinder. Not only is this a very tidy and stock-appearing installation, it's also much easier to find 1932 pedals than it is to locate a set from a 1939 Ford. We've included a pattern for the master cylinder mount made from 1/4-inch steel plate.

Modifying the 1932 Brake Pedal

The brake arm is removed from the top of the pedal body, chamfered to a V, and either TIG or MIG welded to the bottom of the pedal, on the flat pad for the grease zerk fitting. The weld should be built up in successive passes for full penetration and strength, then blended smooth to eliminate any sharp breaks or ridges. A new grease zerk port is then drilled and tapped next to the arm.

Master Cylinder Installation

The hot-setup master cylinder is the 1939–1948 passenger-car piece. As with wheel cylinders, you can rebuild an old master cylinder just as long as its bore isn't badly pitted or scored. You can also spend a great deal of time looking for a cylinder that's in good condition, however, which prompts us to suggest you buy a new or professionally rebuilt unit. Check in your Ford parts catalogs.

With our brake system using 1932 pedals, the master cylinder attaches directly to the bracket that's bolted to the 1932 K-member. The pedal arm was repositioned to the bottom of the pedal, as shown in the accompanying illustration, so its force is transmitted rearward, to the master cylinder. The pedal-to-master cylinder pushrod is made from a 7/16-inch x 3-1/2-inch bolt trimmed and shaped to fit into the bore in the master cylinder piston. A Ford brake clevis and a jam nut connect it to the pedal, permit freeplay adjustment throughout a range of about 1/2 inch, and hold it in place once adjustment is correct.

Plumbing the Brake System

Three flexible hoses are required for plumbing the brakes, plus 12 feet of 1/4-inch brake line for the rear brakes and 7 feet of 3/16-inch line for the front brakes. You'll also need a Y fitting for the rear, a Tee for the master cylinder, and another Tee for the front brakes, plus a half-dozen small Adel clamps.

Since the rear brake lines are mounted on the radius rods and move up and down with the rear end, they can be hard-mounted to the wheel cylinders and to a fixed Y block toward the front

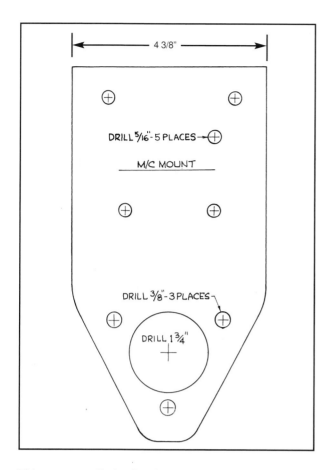

DRILL 5/16"- 5 PLACES →

M/C MOUNT

DRILL 3/8"- 3 PLACES

DRILL 1 3/4"

4 3/8"

This master cylinder bracket is made of 1/4-inch steel plate and is designed for the '32 pedal assembly. It bolts to the backside of a '32 cross-member and mounts a rear-facing 1939–1948 Ford master cylinder. Photocopy the image, enlarge to the 4 3/8-inch dimension shown, and use for a pattern.

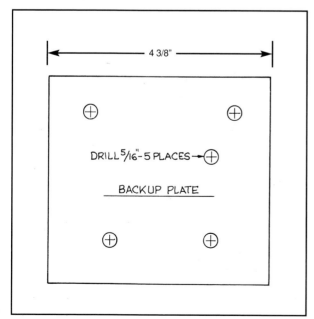

4 3/8"

DRILL 5/16"- 5 PLACES →

BACKUP PLATE

Hard lines for the rear brakes follow radius rods from the wheel cylinders to a Y-block that's located on the torque tube, needing no flex lines. Lines are held in place with Adel clamps.

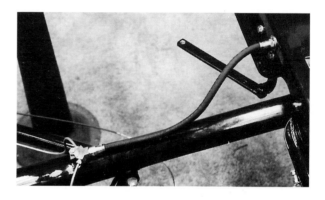

Rear brake hard lines end at the Y-block on the torque tube. A single flex hose is bulkheaded into the original Model A cross-member, where it connects to a short hard line to the master cylinder.

A single hard line from the master cylinder connects to a bulkhead T-fitting, to which the left-front brake hose and the crossover hard line for the opposite wheel are connected. The crossover line ends in a bulkhead fitting that's connected to the right brake flex hose.

A 1932 Ford parking brake lever is mounted on a simple angle-iron bracket held in place with transmission cover bolts.

of the torque tube. A flex line from the Y block to a secured hard line that connects to the master cylinder provides required movement between the frame and rear suspension.

There are two sections of hard line for the front brakes—one from the master cylinder to a Tee at the left flex line, and one from the Tee, across the front cross-member, to the right flex line.

The bulkhead ends of the front flex lines are connected to the frame rails through 1/2-inch-diameter holes drilled 18 to 19 inches back from the end of the front frame horns. The flex lines themselves should be 15 to 16 inches long to accommodate the full range of steering.

Filling and Bleeding the System

No matter how careful your prepaint brake system work is, it's essential to check the all-new system once everything is connected for the last time, before you put the car on the road. Look for and correct leaks, and make sure everything works the way it's supposed to. To prevent correctable leaks from damaging any of that wonderful, fresh paint, we suggest you fill, bleed, and check the system with noncorrosive DOT-5 silicone brake fluid. Once you're satisfied everything's OK, purge the system and refill it with that great old eat-your-paint DOT-4 stuff by filling and bleeding the entire system once again. Or you could just forget about it and operate with the silicone stuff—not totally correct, but who's going to know?

Parking Brake—Clean, Simple, and Ford

Old-Ford parking brakes, from Model A through 1936, couldn't be simpler, with a ratcheted direct-pull lever bolted on the transmission right next to the gear selector. Since the 1937-and-later transmission case doesn't have any provisions for the early brake, you'll need to make a simple bracket to mount the handle and ratchet. We made ours from a short length of 2 x 2-inch angle iron and welded 1/2-inch standoffs to the face of the bracket and captive nuts to the backside to make it easy to install the lever assembly. Now, if all this is too much hot-rodding for you, Specialty Ford Parts makes a neat bracket like the one just described.

To continue with our park brake scheme, an adjustable rod connects to a drawbar that's pivoted from a bracket bolted to the original Model A center cross-member, and a clevis connects the drawbar to the cable equalizer.

With the rear brakes assembled, the parking brake cables are connected and routed along the rear radius rods. Most cables used with Bendix brakes are similar to those on our Lincoln brakes and require a fixed locator to prevent the cable sheath from moving when the cable is pulled to set the brakes.

The parking brake cables for 1939–1948 Ford passenger car brakes are unsheathed and can run straight from the brakes to the equalizer.

WHEELS—THE LOOK STARTS HERE

Wheels—along with tires—are one of the stronger visual elements on any car. On a small highboy roadster they all but take control of the car's character and presence.

Wheel options on the postwar cars were limited to spokes or solids. Even so, planning and care are required to ensure the right look.

Ford spoke wheels are as handsome as they can be. They're not quite as tough as the Kelsey-Hayes wire wheels, however, and weren't as popular with hot-rodders in the past.

Kelsey-Hayes spokers were the hot setup for prewar hot rods. Stronger than the original Ford wheels, they were relegated to second-class status with the advent of the solid-center Ford wheel in 1940.

Not popular with straightline hot-rodders, the 1936–1939 Ford wide-five (referring to the large-diameter bolt pattern) wheel was the first choice for many forms of circle-track racing. Truth to tell, it's a great-looking hot rod wheel as well

Our favorite postwar hot rod front wheel—the 4x16-inch 1940 Ford. Shod with a 16-inch motorcycle tire or a small automobile tire, it's as good as it ever got! We'll pass on the cycle tires, however, for normal driving.

Our Buick look-alike rear wheel is made from a fresh 15-inch rim and a Ford center. An original 1949–1950 Ford stainless steel trim ring and a repro 1942 hubcap, plus original style accent stripes complete the classic postwar look.

This 5.50x16-inch front passenger car tire looks great, and it has a larger, more realistic flat contact patch than a motorcycle tire.

Spokes—Classic but a Bit Long in the Tooth
By the time Johnny came marching home the second time, spokes were on the way out as Ford solids became the predominant wheel design. Still, there were a number of cars in that era rolling on spokers and looking just great.

There were essentially two hot-rod spoke wheels, the OEM Ford wheel and the Kelsey-Hayes wheel. Both were manufactured in 16-inch diameters with 4- to 5-inch rim widths. The Ford wheel has straight-pull spokes while the K-H spokes are longer and angled in a pronounced cross-over pattern. The K-H wheel is stronger than the Ford and consequently was the preferred wheel among racers and hot rodders, but there's no denying that the Ford wheel is a handsome, even graceful piece of work.

Widened K-H wheels can be found today, as well as 15-inch versions, and they offer great potential for creating a stylized dirt-tracker look. Be careful, however; there's a fine line between a nostalgia performance look and a whimsical caricature.

The safest—and the purest application of Kelseys on a street-driven hot rod—are unfettled 16-inchers at all four corners, brightly painted and fitted with polished trim rings and hub caps, and shod with the extremes of big 'n little rubber. With spokers, it don't get no better than this!

Solids—Still the Right New Look
Ford solid-center wheels were the hot setup the moment they were introduced on the 1940 models. With plated hubcaps and stainless-steel trim rings against body-color or contrasting paint,

they were and are one of the more handsome automobile wheels ever styled and manufactured.

Our favorite front wheel is a popular carryover from the postwar hot rod—the prewar 1940 16-incher. It was a one-year wheel in that it had the new five-on 5 1/2-inch bolt pattern and a 4-inch-wide rim; rim width increased to 4 1/2 and 5 inches the next year.

The 1940 wheel willingly accommodates tires as large as 6.00x16, but it's at its hod-rodding best when it's hugged with a 5.00x16 tire. Later 16-inch passenger car wheels grew no wider than 5 inches and still handle narrow front tires OK, but not as well as the 1940 wheel.

As rear wheels, the "wider" 16-inchers begin to look a bit narrow as tire sizes approach 7.00x16, although they're correct for an early car and begin to look pretty good after a while; it's just a matter of reprogramming because we've had a couple of decades of wide wheels and fat tires to condition us to the big-footprint look.

The hot setup years ago was a 15-inch Buick rim on a Ford wheel center. The wide—by 1950s standards—Buick rim measured only 6 1/2 inches but looked a foot wide to us at the time. Rather than hunt for a pair of old Buick wheels today, we simply bought a pair of new 7-inch-wide 15-inch rims and fitted them to Ford centers. We increased the offset by 1 inch over stock to mimic the Buick-rim look. Also, the added backspace puts the rear tires a little closer to the body on the wider-than-stock 1940 Ford rear end.

You can make up your wheels yourself, using a spindle and hub mounted in a vise as a fixture, with a dial indicator to measure the runout, or you can entrust the work to a wheel shop. This is a simple task for a pro and should cost about 20 bucks a wheel.

TIRES—
RIGHT RUBBER FOR THE RIGHT LOOK
Big 'n little rubber has been an essential hot rod element since early dry-lakes racing. Big rear tires were a quick route to higher gearing on the characteristically low-geared old Ford differentials, and the tall "skins" rapidly became popular on the streets of southern California both for their appearance and their performance. The majority of hot rods in the postwar era were daily drivers, and the long legs the big tires gave them improved driveability and fuel economy.

Small front tires, really small 5.00x16 motorcycle hides from Harleys and Indians, came on strong in the late 1940s, a carryover from the dry lakes where the small contact patch meant low rolling resistance. As great as they look, we don't recommend them for general use because they aren't designed for use on automobiles. A far better choice is a 5.50x16 or 6.00x16 passenger car tire.

Fine-texture tread and edge fluting on the Firestone Deluxe Champion make this one of the handsomest of hot rod rear tires.

Wide whites look terrific, but they seriously alter the character of a car from hot rod to cruiser. Their popularity grew as the 1950s wore on and the early cars were "retired" in favor of later models.

The Bias-Ply Profile—Right On Target

For our perfect SoCal dry lakes look, we first chose 5.10x16 motorcycle rubber for the front and a classic pair of 7.00x15 Firestone Deluxe Champions for the rear—both bias-ply construction with the appropriate cross-section.

By the time we had logged 5,000 miles in the roadster, the front tires developed an odd wear pattern and began deteriorating rapidly. We switched to a 4.50/4.75x16 Firestone Deluxe Champion passenger car tire that is quieter, provides a more comfortable ride and noticeably better handling, and appears to have twice the tread life as the motorcycle tires—with far greater peace of mind.

At about 12,000 miles we swapped the 7.00x15 rear tires and wheels for a pair of 7.00x16 'Stones on Lincoln wheels for purely cosmetic reasons. The fat 15-inch tires looked fatter each day, and way out of time with the roadster. The 16s are taller by more than 2 inches and just enough skinnier to look extra correct. We think the Firestone Deluxe Champion is one of the handsomest tires ever produced. And, it's available at around $90 apiece in blackwall, or just more than $100 in wide whites, from Coker Tire (see Appendix A).

Coker has a great selection of narrow 16-inch passenger car tires in 4.50-4.75, 5.00-5.25, and 5.50 tread sizes from both Firestone and B.F.Goodrich, along with comparable widths in 15-inch diameter, also in blackwall and wide whitewalls.

The Radial Connection—
Bulgies Have Their Good Points, But . . .

As sweet and correct as the old bias-ply tires look on traditional hot rods, radial tires are hard to kick, habit-wise, particularly for hot rods that are driven a lot. You already know about the radial benefits, and the only complaint we've heard is that they don't look quite right, but this is usually because the tire is the wrong aspect ratio—sidewall height-to-tread width.

The 50- and 60-series radials are indeed too short and fat for old hot rods, 70-series tires are acceptable, and 75-series radials are just fine.

For the front, 155R to 195R look pretty good, and there are even some 16-inch radials available in 175R and 185R. Blackwall radials are abundant, and Coker is making wide-white radials—in 75 series, thank you, Coker—just for folks like us.

But they still bulge.

Chapter 6

THE ENGINE

HENRY'S FLATHEAD V-8:
HIGH PERFORMANCE FOR THE COMMON MAN

Few new engines have been as quickly embraced by hot-rodders as was Henry's V-8 in 1932. Deuce roadsters were racing—and winning—as soon as their fenders could be unbolted. To put matters into historical perspective, even the ubiquitous Chevy V-8 was a bit of a snail in its acceptance as the new standard in the mid-1950s when compared with the original Ford flathead V-8. But then the Chevy wasn't all that unusual in its time; there were a half-dozen affordable OHV engines that preceded it, while in 1932 the Ford V-8 was a unique and exciting piece of hardware at a budget price.

Not only was the Ford the first low-cost production V-8 engine, it was an engine that pushed the manufacturing envelope so far out of shape that a fresh envelope had to be created, in the form of all-new foundry technology. To give it its full due, this wonderful little motor forever changed the direction of automobile engine design and manufacturing in the United States and established the baseline that all other manufacturers would eventually have to step up to.

What made the Ford V-8 affordable was also what made it revolutionary: It was a unitized engine with crankcase and cylinder banks cast as one piece. V-8s and other V arrangements that preceded it were expensive built-up engines with crankcases and cylinder blocks cast separately, machined, and then bolted

The right hardware, correct preparation, and meticulous assembly result in healthy and long-lived "flatmotors" that dispel the old-Ford myths and return countless hours for your efforts.

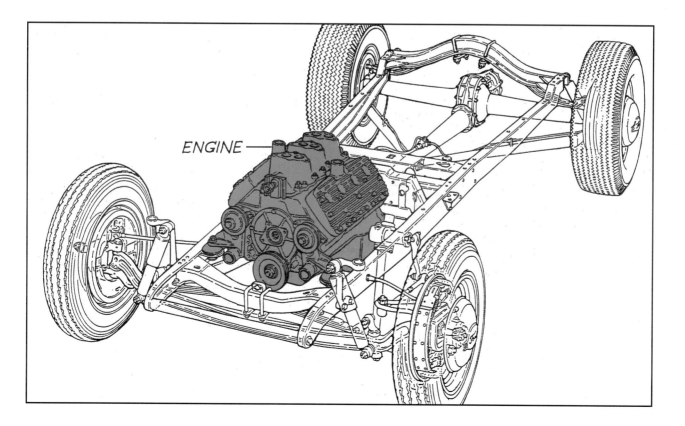

ENGINE —

together. The foundry technology that made the Ford V-8 possible didn't even exist prior to the development of this inexpensive, successful production engine.

After more than two decades of almost uncontested domination of hot-rodding, the Ford flathead began to lose ground to the potentially more-powerful overheads in the early 1950s, and by the end of that decade the flathead was well on its way out as a major player. Some of the top-running, hard-core adherents who refused to give up on the L-heads were still dusting the newer engines, but the battle grew increasingly tough for the old Fords as the burgeoning aftermarket industry focused its resources on developing hardware for the overheads.

While many rodders didn't take the time to learn how to correctly spec and build a flatmotor, ignorance and youthful incompetence are conveniently forgotten now when we look back on those early days, and the flatmotor itself gets all the blame for boilovers and breakdowns. Never mind the thousands of great-running, race-winning, record-setting flathead V-8s that stoked the creative fires in a couple of generations of inquisitive, inventive minds. In plain fact, the flathead responds like any other good engine to skilled, knowledgeable building.

We're not going to cover a detailed step-by-step engine buildup here because that's a book in itself. Instead, we recommend several excellent books to guide you through the nuts 'n bolts work required to put together a first-class flatmotor while we provide our own touches, tips, and direction to help make your flatmotor strong and special. This chapter will also not cover intake manifolds; they're discussed in detail with the fuel system in chapter 10.

For basic flatmotor mechanical work we recommend Ron Bishop's *Rebuilding the Famous Ford Flathead* (see Appendix A). This book covers disassembly, cleaning, inspection, and assembly, and relates the work to current practices and services. You'll want the latest edition, because flatmotor prices have been climbing rapidly in the last few years and the prices reflected in earlier printings of the book are disarmingly low.

We also recommend Ron Holleran's *Nostalgia—Rebuilding and Modifying the Flathead Ford V-8*. While Ron Bishop's book is written from the perspective of a restorer, Ron Holleran's point-of-view is that of a veteran hot-rodder—a builder of circle-track flatmotors who also understands what's needed for the street and what's to be avoided. Holleran has some wonderful ideas and insights, and his book is essential for the flatmotor builder's library, plus it's a good read.

And be sure to include Tex Smith's *The Complete Ford Flathead V-8 Engine Manual* in your library. Lots of great information and another good read.

For our part, we're about to show you how to spec a strong, reliable street motor, where to find everything you need, and how to put it all together in a trouble-free flatmotor that looks great, sounds great, and is fun to drive.

FORD'S FLATHEAD FAMILY

During its 21 years of production, the Ford flathead evolved in such a way that distinct features and specifications overlap from one "series" to the next, making it tough for the uninitiated to identify the great years from the merely good ones. Let's begin by unraveling the skein, so you'll be sure to start with the engine you need.

1932–1936—
21 Studs and Water Pumps in the Heads

All of Henry's V-8s are to be cherished, some more so than others, however. The first five years of production, characterized by water pump heads, are best left to the restorers. Not only is speed equipment virtually nonexistent today for these very early motors, but they cost as much to build as the later ones with far less horsepower return for the dollar.

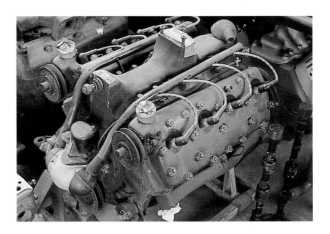

The 1932–1936 Ford flathead motor is strictly for the restorers. The key distinguishing features are the water pumps mounted on the heads.

1937–1938—
21 Studs and Water Pumps in the Block

In terms of real-world performance and reliability in a street-driven A-V8 roadster, the later 21-stud engine is acceptable and usually quite affordable; it's not uncommon to find complete, reasonably fresh engines in the $300–$600 range harvested

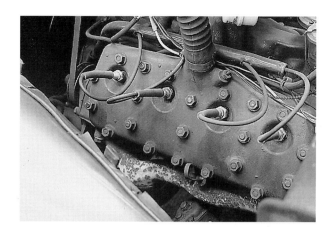

The 1937–1938 motor is starting to look like the real thing, with its water pumps mounted on the block. The 21 studs on each head are a dead giveaway that this one's not quite there, although a good-running take-out from a restored car can be a very respectable budget street motor.

The 1939–1942 Ford 21A motors are fully fledged 24-stud flatheads and will accept all the aftermarket speed goodies you can hang on 'em.

from restored 1937 and 1938 cars that are about to become street rods. And as a bonus, it will probably have a perfectly good transmission attached to it!

The principal drawback to a 21-stud engine is the shortage of external speed equipment. While the camshaft design is the same from 1932 to 1953, intake manifolds and heads are not interchangeable, and so the reproduction hardware that's being manufactured today won't fit 1937 and 1938 engines. Intake manifolds for 21-stud engines show up at swap meets, and in good condition they're perfectly serviceable. Vintage high-performance heads are rare and rarer still in useable condition. An acceptable alternative—then as now—is milling of stock heads (0.090-inch for flattop pistons, 0.060-inch for domed pistons) to increase the compression ratio, and a set of chrome acorn covers for the head nuts or bolts. If you have a good 21-stud engine you want to use, get intimate with *Hemmings Motor News*. We've seen NOS unfinned aluminum Ford heads selling for about the same as a set of finned heads for the later engines. When polished and tarted up with chrome acorn nut covers, the new/old Ford heads look great.

If you're building an early engine, you'll have to refer to Ron Bishop's and Tex Smith's books almost entirely for assembly and detail information. We have barely enough space to cover the later engines that dominated postwar hot-rodding.

Finally, don't expect to coax the same levels of performance from the old engines as you'll find with the later ones. In spite of their look-alike nature, the old fellows can't be upgraded with most of the later, power-producing hardware.

1939–1942—
24 Studs and Water Pumps in the Block

Now we're getting somewhere. When Ford introduced the Mercury in 1939, hot-rodding was given a major boost with some improved engine architecture. The new Mercury was treated to the first "full-size" flathead with a 3 3/16-inch bore, while the Ford was kept at 3 1/16 inch. Although the Ford version was still not quite fully evolved as far as hot-rodding was concerned, it was and is a marvelous little street motor.

Commonly referred to as the 21A, the Ford motors are reasonably plentiful, sell for less than the Mercury and later motors, and—best of all—accept all the later speed equipment. Fully dressed, the 21A is virtually undetectable by all but the hardest-cored old Forders.

The Mercury motor for 1939–1942 is designated 99A. Large Ford trucks had a virtually identical motor designated 99T. The 99 blocks, with a larger bore, were more robust in the cylinder area and have long been considered the ultimate flathead racing block. They've been sought for years and only rarely does a virgin casting show up today. They're identified by large, keystone-shaped water transfer passages between the center cylinders, like those on the later 8BA blocks. Many 99 blocks also have a raised intake deck that follows the outline of the manifold.

Later Flathead V-8s—
59A and 8BA/CM

The final two series of flatheads—the 59A (1946–1948) and 8BA(Ford)/CM (Mercury) (1949–1953)—are the stuff of which most postwar hot rods were made. The blocks for these two

The 1939–1942 99A Mercury and 99T truck motors have a larger bore and heftier cylinder walls. This is the ultimate race motor foundation. Look for the keystone-shaped water passages between the bores.

By 1946, the flathead was well evolved, and Fords and Mercurys were essentially the same. The centered coolant spigot in the cylinder heads and integral bell housing are identifiers, along with a cast "59" on most bellhousings.

series are strong and architecturally quite similar, but with several important differences. The 59 block has an integral bellhousing, while the 8BA/CM uses a separate stamped-steel bellhousing, which makes it more versatile with regard to transmission selection. The coolant inlets in 59-series engines are in the center of the heads, and in the 8BA/CM they are at the front of the heads. The more traditional appearing 59-series heads

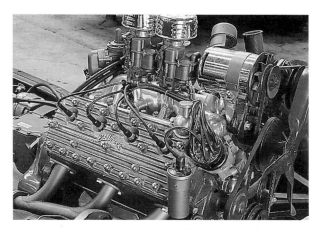

The Ford 8BA and Mercury CM motors were introduced in 1949 and are easily recognized by their front water spigots, bevel-gear offset distributor, and stamped bell housing.

can be used on an 8BA/CM block, as long as some of the water passages in the block are first plugged. Conversely, late heads can be used on the early block if the front center hole in each head is plugged.

The 59-series engine retained floating rod bearings, and the 8BA/CM had modern locked-insert bearings. The crankshafts are otherwise interchangeable. More on this later. Even the 8BA/CM bevel-gear offset distributor is a work-around item that can be retained or replaced. Most important for the 59A and 8BA/CM blocks is that they accommodate the full range of fun-and-games ideas and hardware that have allowed these wonderful little bent-eights to capture and hold speed and racing records long after they should have been relegated to scrap. So say some.

WHAT TO LOOK FOR

Our favorite block for a street motor—and the one we used for the B-T Highboy—is a 59 series, and the best candidate will have a stock bore and no obvious damage or cracks. Pay particular attention to the area around the valves—between adjacent valve pockets and between valve pockets and the cylinder—because this is where debilitating cracking is most likely to occur. Unless the block is certified to be OK, insist on a return privilege if it turns out to be unusable. You may have to absorb the cost of Magnaflux and pressure-test inspection—usually about $100–$150—but it's excellent insurance.

While it's possible to repair cracks in the cylinder decks with pinning or welding, the work is highly specialized and expensive—and best avoided.

Our first-choice crankshaft, which we used, is a 1949–1953 Mercury casting, which has 1/4 inch more stroke than its Ford counterpart. Look for the characteristic 5/8-inch cleanout hole in

The Mercury CM 4.0-inch stroke crankshaft has a 5/8-inch cleanout hole in each journal. Those in Ford cranks are 3/8 inch.

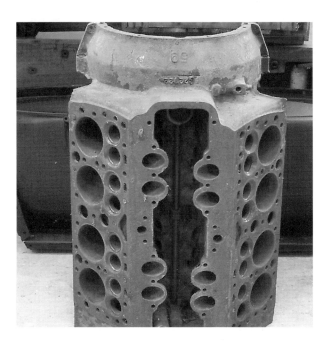

After cleaning and Magnaflux inspection, the block should be sent to the metal stripper for a thorough acid cleaning to remove rust and scale from the water jackets.

each journal. The 3/8-inch hole in the 3 3/4-inch-stroke Ford crank is noticeably smaller.

There's nothing wrong with the shorter-stroke Ford crankshaft, but the Merc's added stroke is like free horsepower with no added effort. True stroker cranks that have had the rod journals offset ground, or even welded and then ground, are more costly and bothersome than they are worth for a street-driven motor.

We think 8BA connecting rods are the better choice of available rods because they are a contemporary locked-insert design. The 21A rods used in 59A and earlier engines use floating full-width bearings that, because of their low demand today, are very expensive.

GETTING READY

The motor work described is either "do" or "buy," depending on your own hands-on experience and tools and equipment. For example, when we recommend that you flash-grind the beams on the connecting rods, it's no big deal if you know how to do it. If you don't, this isn't the time to learn. Save that for your next project and ask your engine-builder for a quote on this task. This is definitely a "buy" decision. Grinding the outside of the block to make it smooth, however, is a "do" task because you don't want to pay shop rate for a job that requires only moderate skill and knowledge.

Cleaning and Inspection

The block must be thoroughly cleaned inside and out to remove grease and grime as well as all traces of scale from the waterjackets—a key starting point for a cool-running flathead, and one that was frequently overlooked in the past. Modern bake-and-blast cleaning will do the job in a single step, giving the casting a foundry-fresh finish inside and out. Have the block magnafluxed after cleaning to ensure it's sound and free of cracks between valve seats and cylinders. Small cracks between water holes in the cylinder decks are not uncommon nor are they anything to worry about.

If hot tanking is the only means of cleaning available to you, have the block metal stripped to remove scale from the water jackets, but only after it's been magnafluxed so you won't waste the cost of stripping a cracked block.

When you get the block back, tumble it over and over on a large plywood panel or a wood deck to further break loose any remaining scale, and prod and blow the scale loose with a long metal tube attached to an air nozzle. Then, flush the cooling jackets with high-pressure water.

The crankshaft should also be thoroughly cleaned and magnafluxed. Make certain the

A few hours spent polishing the outside of the block creates a great background for polished aluminum and chrome. The stock heads and manifold "mask" the mating surfaces and engine interior during painting.

Old bearings are taped in place on the crankshaft journals to prevent damage during grinding and polishing of the counterweights.

plugs are removed from the crankshaft so the sludge traps can be thoroughly cleaned. Otherwise, sludge and metal shavings may be loosened during cleaning but not flushed away. If it's not removed, you can count on it finding its way into the lubrication system later on, damaging bearings and quite probably the crankshaft. And don't rely on Welch plugs to block the sludge-trap holes; have them tapped and blocked with screw-in plugs.

Grinding and Polishing
This is the time to do all of the hand work on the block—intake and exhaust porting and polishing, plus polishing the outside, should you care to. We recommend the external cleanup because the engine is so visible, and a smooth, glossy flat-motor block is a great background for polished aluminum heads and manifold.

You might also consider grinding and polishing the crankshaft counterweights to lighten the rotating mass and to make it move more easily through the oil atmosphere inside the engine. While not essential for a street engine, the work contributes to snappier throttle response and more power. Before grinding on the crankshaft, duct tape old bearings over the journals to prevent them from being damaged.

Flash grind the beams of the connecting rods to remove any roughness, and grind off the ears on the small end. But don't get carried away; these little beauties are already pretty light and don't have much unnecessary meat on them.

Machining
Cart the block, crankshaft, connecting rods, a new set of pistons, the flywheel, and clutch to that flatmotor-friendly machine shop you found for the critical work, which includes:
- Bore and hone the cylinders
- Deck and surface the block
- Check the crankshaft and turn if needed
- Install camshaft bearings
- Magnaflux, straighten, resize, and rebush connecting rods
- Balance

Here's a piece of advice that's worth the price of this book: Engine balancing is not optional. A professional balancing job on the crankshaft, connecting rods, and pistons, plus flywheel and clutch, is essential for a strong, smooth-running, long-lived flatmotor.

If your goal is a cosmetically correct A-V8 roadster with better-than-stock performance, have the block bored no more than necessary to clean up and true the cylinders. One of hot-rodding's engine-building constants tells us that the larger the bore, the thinner the cylinder wall, and

The 21A connecting rod on the left uses full-floating bearings (shown), while the 8BA/CM rod uses modern locked insert bearings.

The venerable Johnson adjustable tappet is lighter than new ones available today, but not easy to find. Keep your eyes open for the little tool that holds the tappet while the adjuster is turned.

The 1949–1953 truck oil pump is readily available brand new, is reasonably priced, and has wholly modern flow and pressure performance levels.

One-piece valve guides are essential. The chamfer at the top of the one shown on the valve improves flow through the port.

the thinner the cylinder wall, the higher the engine temperature. And while we're going to tell you how to make your flatmotor a cool runner, there's no sense borrowing trouble.

If you want to experience the total magic of a built, streetable flatmotor, however, a 3/16-inch overbore is in order. This yields a 3 3/8-inch bore, which is still a reasonable oversize in a good block—plus, it provides the important bore component for bench-racing stories, as in "This baby's a three-eighths by three-eighths." And while undersquare flatmotors wake up real quick with a bit more piston area for the combustion charge to

push down on, the larger bores tend to run warmer at low speed.

Align boring the mains is probably not necessary, as long as the crank is true and will coast when spun with new bearings clearanced at 0.002–0.003 inch. Unless you're an obsessed engine builder who has to check each step personally, entrust this judgment call to the machine shop, or be prepared to cart the engine home and back a couple of extra times.

Today's unleaded fuels dictate the need for hardened valve seats, and for the 59A engine builder the good news is that the block already has hard Stellite seats. Phased out in late 8BA production, the old seats may be worn beyond service limits at this point, in which case they must be replaced. And you might as well replace them with 1.6-inch seats in the intake tract so you can use inexpensive 1.6-inch Chevy stainless-steel valves. The larger seats don't cost any more, and new Chevy valves are cheaper than the old Ford replacements. And if that's not enough inducement, the larger valves improve intake flow and performance.

MAKING THE RIGHT CHOICES

Recall that we're not going to take you by the hand and walk you through engine assembly; that's what those other books are for. But we want to share some important points and make some recommendations born from years of building countless flatheads in the old shop in the orchard.

Before you do anything else to that crisp, fresh block, chase all the threads with taps to re-

Exhaust port dividers are installed in the shared exhaust passage between the center cylinders to prevent the exhaust charge from one cylinder diluting the intake charge of the adjacent cylinder.

move burrs and any remaining scale. For this job you'll need:

- 1/4-20 tap
- 5/16-24 tap
- 3/8-16 tap
- 1/2-18 tap

When the block and all the threads are clean, scour the block with hot soapy water and stiff brushes, then thoroughly dry it with lint-free rags and air and give it a good dousing with WD-40 to keep it from rusting.

Install new cylinder head studs in the block, set in Permatex. Later, when you install the heads, apply a generous coat of antiseize compound to the entire shoulder area of each stud so the heads can be easily removed at the next valve service or rebuild.

As a last block-prep step, install exhaust port dividers between the center pair of cylinders on each bank to prevent exhaust gases from diluting the intake charge in the adjacent cylinder. Baffles are available from flathead-friendly sources like Speedway Motors.

The Right Oil Pump

Unless you have a wonderful old Melling high-performance pump in a box on the shelf, you'll have to "settle" for a new 1949–1953 truck pump from one of the flatmotor parts suppliers like Patrick's (see Appendix A). This is an excellent pump, reasonably priced, and well suited to high-performance flathead duty.

The Right Pistons

Good-quality cast pistons are excellent for a street motor. Patrick's has four-ring pistons for well under $200 a set, and Speedway stocks cast three-ring pistons for about $230. If you just have to have something high-tech, Ross makes an excellent forged piston, and Egge Machine has a new hypereutectic piston that should fill the bill.

The 12-hole timing gear on the left is no longer made, but it's important only if you are super-fussy about cam timing on a street motor.

These high-silicon cast pistons are light and as strong as most forged pistons, but have a low co-efficient of expansion that permits them to be fitted with 0.002–0.003-inch clearance for low noise and decreased oil consumption.

We recommend use of good quality cast iron or chrome-moly piston rings, like those from Sealed Power. Chrome-plated rings sound like a great idea, but they are too hard and totally unnecessary for what will probably be a low-time street motor. Cast iron rings seat quickly; chrome-moly rings take a little longer, while chrome-plated rings can take several thousand miles to seat, if they ever do. And be sure to follow the ring manufacturer's instructions for honing, fit, and break-in.

The Right Valvetrain

Fit those new 1.6-inch Chevy intake and 1.5-inch Ford exhaust valves to the later style one-piece valve guides, and use new rubber seals on the intakes. Before you do this, however, chamfer the ends of the guides to help the flow through the ports.

Since flatmotors are not winders—not even built ones—there's no need for heavy spring pressure. New Lincoln Zephyr-type springs—the original hot setup—are available from Red's Headers. Likewise, Isky springs will handle the valve-closing chores with an acceptable level of pressure (see Appendix A).

Isky also continues to grind some of the best-ever flatmotor cams. For street applications, we like both the 3/4-race Max 1 and the 400 Jr. The milder Max 1 scarcely lopes at idle, and it's a good fuel-mileage grind in spite of a noticeable performance improvement. But for our money, the 400 Jr. with its great snap and rumpety idle is the cam to have. The fuel-economy penalty of a few miles per gallon is easily offset by much stronger acceleration than the Max 1, and of course there's that wonderful sound!

We'd be remiss if we didn't acknowledge that there are other excellent camshafts available for the flathead. Like political and religious convictions, camshaft preferences are closely and passionately held and it would be folly to fail to recognize the existence today of some of the heavy hitters from the past. A full line-up of both Potvin and Schneider camshafts are available from Flathead Jack (see Appendix A), and you may want to talk to him about specs and performance before making your selection. The flathead cam wars of the 1950s live on into the new millennium!

The best lifter is still the old lightweight Johnson adjustable tappet, and it's too bad they are no longer made. Serviceable Johnsons show up at swap meets, however. When you buy that old stock motor that you're going to massage into shape you may find it already has a set of Johnsons. They were favored by a lot of engine rebuilders because they

This race motor crank has the ultimate whittling and polishing job. There's no need to go quite this far for a street motor, but we included it to illustrate the possibilities if one is willing to invest the time.

make valve adjustment so easy. The newer, heavier adjustable lifters also work fine, and are available from flathead parts sources.

Also readily available is a new aluminum timing gear to replace the fiber gear on the cam. The new gears have four holes, which pretty much locks you into a single timing setup. If you're super critical about cam timing, look for an old 12-hole gear at swap meets. Good ones show up all the time, and they'll allow you to precisely degree the cam to crank position.

The Right Cylinder Heads

The use of old aluminum cylinder heads is risky. Damage from electrolysis and erosion is a certainty, and even when it's repairable the cost is usually more than the heads are worth—maybe as much as a new set. And, without precise measurement, you don't know how much material has been removed from the sealing surface and the combustion chambers. Imagine the fun you'd have with a pair of heads that have been whittled to a compression ratio of about 13:1!

For our money, new cylinder heads are essential to a trouble-free flatmotor. The two most-popular new heads are from Offenhauser and Edelbrock, available through many old Ford parts sources (see Appendix A). Offenhauser heads are marked with the amount of valve lift they will accommodate—0.375-, 0.400-, or 0.425-inch, eliminating any guesswork about which head you need. Edelbrock heads are marked with compression ratio. This is a little less precise, but all that matters is that 8:1 Edelbrocks will accommodate 0.400 inch of valve lift—just what's needed for an Isky 400-Jr. or Potvin 400 cam.

Barney Navarro is also still making cylinder heads in the same high quality that they have always been. They're available direct from Barney (see Appendix A), but order well in advance because he does only a couple of casting runs each year. Also, he'll need to know how much valve lift you're running to ensure sufficient clearance.

The Right Ignition

A fresh and perfect 1946 to 1948 distributor, converted to 12 volts with 12-volt coil and condenser, and a new 1942 "crab" cap is an excellent traditional ignition system for a street-driven flatmotor. We feel that the new Mallory dual-point and electronic distributors that are available from Patrick's as well as several other sources shown in Appendix A are an excellent and reasonable compromise. We chose the dual-point model for our roadster but were tempted by the electronic number because Mallory has gone the extra yard and located the brain inside the distributor, eliminating the need for a remote

The electrolysis in this old aluminum head is minimal, but it appears to have been milled a time or two, making compression ratio a big question.

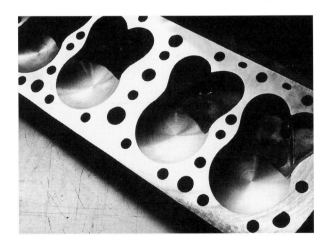

Possibly the ultimate streetable head is the Navarro, designed for use with pop-up domed pistons. If this one catches your fancy, plan on spending some phone time with Barney to work out setup and tuning details.

black-box. No matter which distributor you choose—original Ford or new Mallory—use the Mallory crab cap. It has brass contacts and is made of a specially compounded plastic so it won't carbon track and misfire like the black after-market caps with aluminum contacts that are common today.

There's really only one spark plug for the flatmotor—the Champion H10. Most auto parts stores still carry them, and you can always count on finding them in garden supply stores because they're a popular choice for lawn mowers.

The Right Flywheel and Clutch
A 9 1/2-inch clutch is all that's needed for a light-weight, street-driven roadster. An 11-inch clutch is not only too heavy, it's unnecessarily stiff.

The roadster's low weight also means you can remove some serious weight from the fly-wheel—12 to 16 pounds—with no ill effects on smooth starts. However, aluminum flywheels go too far. They're too light for street duty, and they're pricey.

THE RIGHT COOLING SYSTEM—
A FLATHEAD PRIORITY
While it doesn't seem possible to have a worth-while dialogue about flatheads without spending a great deal of time on the subject of engine cool-ing, we'll try; it's not all that mysterious, and you've already taken the first important step when you thoroughly cleaned the water jacketing and passages in the block.

Water Pumps
A lot of the overheating trouble blamed on flat-heads is attributable to worn bushings and seal

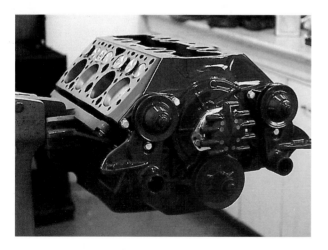

The new Mallory dual-point ignition from Patrick's is excellent and very correct appearing. The electronic version looks essentially the same.

packing in old water pumps that would allow water to leak out almost as fast as you could fill the radiator. Fresh water-tight water pumps are essential to a trouble-free motor, and with new sealed ball-bearing pumps available at about $130–$140 a pair, it makes little sense to mess around with old bushed pumps and their fragile packing seals. The new pumps are available for both 59A and 8BA series engines, all with wide belt sheaves to accommodate the early crank, generator, and fan pulleys.

If you insist on using used bushed passenger car pumps, start fresh with new bushings and seals. Make sure the oil-feed holes in the block and the pumps are clear so they'll have a steady oil supply or they'll quickly fail. During installa-tion, take care to keep the gasket and gasket sealer from blocking the oil-feed holes.

Don't overdo the tension on the drivebelt. Too much tension can shorten the life of the bearings in later style pumps and is a certain way to rapidly wear out the bushings and seals in early pumps, re-sulting in leakage and likely damage to the shafts.

Finally, a common old "cure" for overheating involved drilling holes in the water pump vanes or removing every other vane to reduce coolant flow. The reasoning behind this idea was that the pumps moved the water through the radiator too quickly for it to be cooled. While some old-timers swear by this fix, others say it has little if any benefit for street-driven motors. We're inclined to side with those who say leave the vanes alone. We've seen an idle and low-speed overheating problem cured by replacing modified impellers with stock units.

Radiator
Rather than fritter around with an original 1932 radiator, we opted for a commercially available new one. Sold by JAMCO, the radiator is config-ured for the 1932 shell but pared down to fit un-der it when the shell has been shortened for use on an A-V8 car. The radiator has all the requisite mounting brackets, just like an original, but it has heavy-duty tanks that permit it to operate at higher, more contemporary pressure levels, along with a large modern core.

Fan
An engine-driven fan is as important to a cool-running flathead as are water-tight water pumps. In addition to some of the stock Ford fans and mounts, Specialty Ford Parts has several that can be adapted to meet a variety of configurations. Don't despair just because you can't find a partic-ular Ford fan that just bolts right on; we're build-ing a hot rod, remember. The fan on the B-T Highboy is the result of hours of cut-and-try work. In its final form it consists of shortened 1937 blades mounted on a V-8-60 pulley fitted to

Our new motor spent about 10 hours on the run-in stand while Vern checked its vital signs and looked for leaks. There weren't any.

All together and ready for installation, the little 286-incher is as handsome as any flatmotor we've seen.

a later hub and supported on the type of bracket that Specialty sells. It works as good as it looks.

During the B-T Roadster's first summer on the road, the motor tended to run too warm—195 to 205 degrees Fahrenheit—in prolonged, slow stop-and-go traffic, but would quickly return to normal—180 degrees—once the car was underway. Cooling system capacity and condition were not the problem because the motor runs at 180 degrees, the set-point of the thermostats, at speeds from the mid 30s to sustained highway cruise, even in 95 to 100 degree summer heat. Part of the problem was airflow through the radiator—corrected by adding a spacer between the fan and the hub to place the fan about 1/4 inch away from the radiator core. This, in combination with a return to stock water pump impellers, ended the problem.

ON THE ROAD

Run a quality multigrade oil—20W-50—and change it every 1,500 miles without fail.

Run 180 degree thermostats, and add a pint of machinist's soluble oil to the engine coolant to prevent electrolysis in the cylinder heads. Do this after any coolant leaks have been corrected; the soluble oil mixture makes a mess of things.

Break in the fresh motor just as you would any other, taking care not to overheat it or run it at a sustained speed for the first few hundred miles.

And, most important of all, enjoy the reality of a well-put-together flatmotor and forget about the old wives' tales and myths.

At home in the blue roadster's engine bay, the fully dressed flathead is the definitive hot rod motivator.

Chapter 7

THE TRANSMISSION

A GEARBOX PRIMER

Some of the most important work you'll do as you build your A-V8 involves the transmission. Ford gearboxes from the 1930s and 1940s were just fine for their intended use and in their time, but compared to modern manual transmissions, Henry's three-speeds are a bit primitive, although certainly no worse than those from the direct competition, Chevy and Plymouth. A transmission represents one of the more significant unit costs of manufacturing a car, and it's fiscal folly to make it a lot better than it has to be. It wasn't just an odd coincidence that three of early hot-rodding's favorite bullet-proof gearboxes—Packard, Buick, and Cadillac/LaSalle three-speeds from the late 1930s—were found in big, powerful cars selling for two to four times the price of a Ford.

But you don't need a LaSalle transmission for your A-V8 if you select the right Ford pieces, assemble them correctly, and treat the gearbox with respect once it's in the car.

Nor do you need a 1939 transmission to ensure you'll have the best-possible hot rod gearbox, although that seems to be the only correct cog collector you'll find in the feature stories in the old rod magazines. The real story is that a 1937–1938 case works just fine because it has a relief in the bottom to clear the large main driven gear on the good cluster that was used through 1948. Just make sure the case has a cast "78" on the bottom-left rear corner.

The Ford three-speed transmission is the model of simplicity, easily rebuilt without the need for special tools or fixtures.

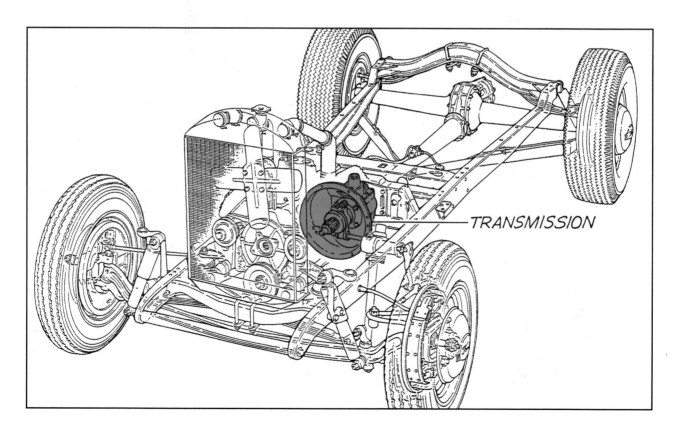

TRANSMISSION

In deference to the advocacy of early rodders and journalists for the 1939 transmission, the 1937–1938 internals aren't all that great mechanically. Today, of course, they're likely to be more worn out than the later sets. But don't pass up a good 1937–1938 case; if not yet like pure gold, they may someday come close.

The best top-shifter transmission, for strength, cost, and availability, is a hybrid that uses a 1939–1949 pickup case and the complete internals from a 1942–1948 passenger car transmission. The pickup case, with a thicker bottom under the relief for the cluster, is stronger than the passenger car case. The pickup gearset, however, is designed for an open driveline, and not all of the pieces will work with a torque tube driveline. Plus, the ratios are a little, well, truck-like. The 1942–1948 passenger car gearsets fit the pickup case perfectly, as well as the 1937–1939 passenger car case. And, they have the latest features and improvements for this transmission design, are more likely to be in better condition than earlier sets, they're plentiful, and they're reasonably priced. Just as important, their ratios are a little better than the earlier passenger car transmissions, although not as well spaced as gotta-have Zephyr gears—the old-Ford equivalent of a close-ratio setup.

Lincoln-Zephyr gears were always pricey, although relatively not nearly so in the past as they are today. And they're not really essential for a first-class rod, although if you have a good set of Zephyrs you've been saving for a project like this one, by all means use them. But rather than shell out an extra $400–$500 on a Zephyr gearset, invest the money in the differential—either a 3.23:1 ring and pinion or some Halibrand quick-change hardware. Your light A-V8 highboy won't need a

stump-puller final drive to get it off the mark and let it accelerate smartly. It will do that quite handily even with tall gearing, and the tall gearing will give your Ford gearset the legs it needs in first and second gears.

Nowhere is it carved in stone that only top shifter transmissions are fit for hot rod duty. Side or column shifters—1940 and later—were almost as desirable and offered a special advantage; legroom in the cockpit for a third passenger or your best girl. If a column shift is for you, you'll need a steering mast jacket and shift rods, preferably from a 1940 passenger car, to go along with that side-shifter transmission.

WHAT TO LOOK FOR

Inspect any candidate transmission carefully. If it's a top shifter, make sure it has the "78" casting number. Remove the shifter cover and check for "mud" in the bottom of the case. A mixture of water, trans-lube, and dirt, this ugly stuff signals that the cluster gear will have pitted teeth where the gears are submerged in it, if the transmission has been sitting for very long.

Check the case for cracks in the front web between the mainshaft bearing bore and the countershaft bore. Under hard acceleration and deceleration, there's a great deal of force applied to the case in this area as the gears try to climb out of mesh with one another. If the case is cracked, it can't hold the gears in perfect mesh. This is a fairly common condition, and expensive to repair.

Inspect the gears and shafts for wear and damage. If more than just a couple of pieces are bad, particularly if the cluster is bad, continue your search for a good transmission.

And while you're searching, keep an eye open for a shifter with two spring-loaded detents, instead of one, for more positive-shifting. Make sure the shifter arms inside the transmission are long enough to engage the gearset. Also make sure the shifter ball and socket are uniformly round. Worn sockets are common and shifters are plentiful, so pass on marginal ones and keep looking for a good one. If the ball and socket are in good shape but the slot for the pivot pin is worn, all you need to do to make shifter action crisp is weld up the slot and recut it to 1/4 inch wide. In any event, use a fresh pin. Vern's favorite pin material is the shank of a tired 1/4-inch drill.

Unless your transmission was recently rebuilt by someone familiar with Ford gearboxes, it should be thoroughly reconditioned as described below. A detailed inspection of the individual elements will tell you what parts are needed, but at a minimum, you'll need a transmission and U-joint gasket set along with new front and rear mainshaft bearings and a fresh front seal.

The "78" casting mark on the rear of this case identifies it as an appropriate candidate for a hot rod top shifter. It's found on 1937–1939 passenger car cases, as well as the stouter 1939–1949 pickup truck top-shift three speeds.

The front web between the mainshaft bearing bore and the countershaft bore is highly stressed under severe abuse, and cracks are not uncommon. A serviceable case must be free of cracks in this critical area.

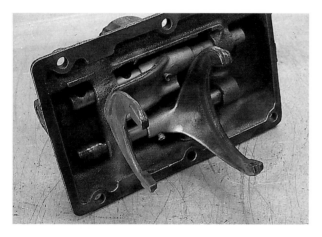

Forks and rods in this double-detent shifter are in excellent shape. Avoid rusted or pitted shafts and bent or badly worn shifters.

Now, a word of advice before you begin: Never strike transmission parts with a steel hammer or hard drifts. Use only brass or bronze hammers and brass drifts. Do otherwise and you can count on damaging good parts.

DISASSEMBLY AND INSPECTION
Be critical when you inspect the transmission, but also be practical. If you've shopped smart, most of the major parts can be reused. When you find borderline parts, however, replace them rather than risk having them fail and ruin other good parts. Virtually all internal bits and pieces for Ford transmissions, including new gears, are available from several of the suppliers listed in Appendix A.

With the big exploded view for reference, take everything apart for a thorough cleaning and detailed inspection:

- Remove the rear mount from the case, pull the cotter pin out of the lock pin for the countershaft/idler shaft, and drive the lock pin out of the case. Then, remove the lock pin from the clutch fork, and drive the fork pivot shaft out of the case.
- Remove the front cover from the case and drive the cluster gear countershaft out of the case with a brass drift.
- Carefully drive the rear bearing off the output shaft with a brass drift. Remove the rear half of the mainshaft assembly from the case.
- Remove the cluster gear assembly from the case and drive out the low/reverse idler gear shaft with a brass drift.
- Check for wear in the case where the countershaft thrust washer makes contact. It's uncommon, but if the thrust washer jams on the shaft, it will wear a recess in the case—reason enough to scrap the case.
- If the synchro rings show any signs of wear, replace them. You should replace the blocks and retainers as well, using the latest block design in place of the earlier ball type.
- Check the synchronizer hub for notches worn into it near the end of the teeth. This condition creates shifting problems and is a reason for replacing the hub.
- Two types of thrust washers were used for the cluster gear, one with lugs and the other with four slots. One works as well as the other, but make sure you replace a worn thrust washer with a new one of the same type.
- Dress all of the mating surfaces on the case, the front cover, and the shifter cover with a large mill-bastard file to remove high spots and ensure leak-free sealing. Dress the throwout sleeve on the front cover with emery cloth and chase all threaded holes with taps.
- If the bearing contacts of the clutch fork are worn flat, carefully dress them so they are smooth and rounded to prevent notchy clutch engagement.
- If the clutch shaft bushings are worn, re-place them. Make sure the grease hole in the bushing lines up with the grease fitting in the case.
- Wear on the clutch shaft occurs on only one side; knock out the lock pin, rotate the shaft 180 degrees, and install a new lock pin.

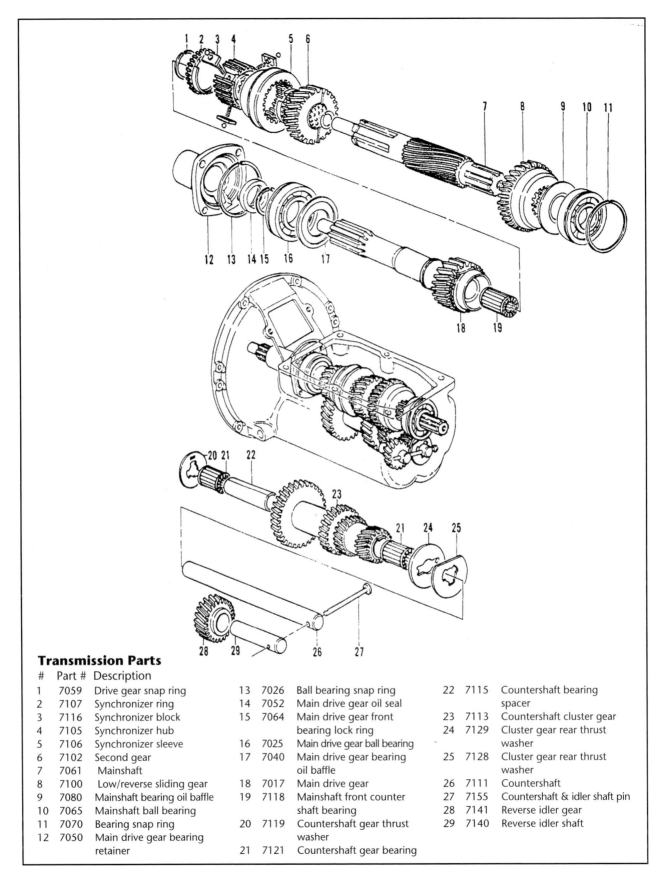

Transmission Parts

#	Part #	Description
1	7059	Drive gear snap ring
2	7107	Synchronizer ring
3	7116	Synchronizer block
4	7105	Synchronizer hub
5	7106	Synchronizer sleeve
6	7102	Second gear
7	7061	Mainshaft
8	7100	Low/reverse sliding gear
9	7080	Mainshaft bearing oil baffle
10	7065	Mainshaft ball bearing
11	7070	Bearing snap ring
12	7050	Main drive gear bearing retainer
13	7026	Ball bearing snap ring
14	7052	Main drive gear oil seal
15	7064	Main drive gear front bearing lock ring
16	7025	Main drive gear ball bearing
17	7040	Main drive gear bearing oil baffle
18	7017	Main drive gear
19	7118	Mainshaft front counter shaft bearing
20	7119	Countershaft gear thrust washer
21	7121	Countershaft gear bearing
22	7115	Countershaft bearing spacer
23	7113	Countershaft cluster gear
24	7129	Cluster gear rear thrust washer
25	7128	Cluster gear rear thrust washer
26	7111	Countershaft
27	7155	Countershaft & idler shaft pin
28	7141	Reverse idler gear
29	7140	Reverse idler shaft

Use this exploded view as your guide when working on the transmission and when ordering replacement parts.

84

TRANSMISSION ASSEMBLY

The Ford three-speed goes together as easily as it comes apart. Just take your time and follow the steps, referring to the illustration, and double check your work as you go.

Use liberal amounts of Lubriplate or an equivalent high-strength assembly lube, as well as transmission lube. Use Permatex No. 2 or an equivalent sealer on the gaskets to reduce the likelihood of leaks and seepage.

- Install the first/reverse idler gear in the case with the lead on the idler teeth facing forward.
- Line up the lock hole in the idler shaft with the holes in the case before pressing the shaft all the way in.
- Liberally coat the front countershaft thrust washer with grease and set it into the case.
- Install the bearings and spacer in the cluster gear with the longer bearing at the front, and set the cluster gear in the case, taking care not to dislodge the thrust washer.
- Assemble the synchronizer. First install the rings in the hub, install the synchronizer blocks, and install the assembled hub in the synchronizer sleeve.
- Use the diagram for guidance, and assemble the rear half of the mainshaft.
- Install the rear half of the mainshaft in the case and add the oil baffle and rear mainshaft bearing.
- Install the rear mount with a gasket, with sealer on both surfaces, and run the bolts in just enough to hold the bearing in place.
- Use the diagram for guidance, and assemble the front half of the mainshaft.
- Install the front half of the mainshaft and the front cover with a new cover gasket, with sealer on both surfaces. Leave the cover bolts loose for now.
- Set the case on the rear mount and install the countershaft from the front of the case. Be patient and work the shaft down through the bearings, spacer, and the cluster until it exits the rear of the case.

- Line up the lock hole in the countershaft with the hole in the case, install the lock pin through both the countershaft and the low/reverse idler gear shaft, and lock the pin in place with a cotter key. Install and tighten the rear bolts and safety wire them in place.
- Tighten the front cover bolts. Install the throwout bearing and carrier, and install the clutch fork on the shaft with a Grade 8 bolt to make future service easier.

When the transmission is fully assembled, bench test it. Turn the input shaft and shift the transmission through all the gears as you watch the output shaft. The output shaft shouldn't turn when the selector is in neutral, but should begin to turn when the transmission is shifted into first gear. And, it should turn faster in second gear than in first, faster in third gear than in second, and it should turn in the opposite direction when it's in reverse.

If the transmission checks out OK, install the U-joint on the output shaft and liberally grease it with Lubriplate. Spread the stuff on like peanut butter on Wonder Bread before adding a layer of sealer to the flange, then a gasket, and finally the inner bell flange after you've liberally laced its sealing surface with silicone.

(The usual—and incorrect—approach to this task is to completely assemble the joint, gaskets, and all, and then "lube" it through the Zerk fitting. It doesn't work that way, folks; the joint doesn't get anywhere near the lubrication it needs and wears out prematurely as a result.)

INSTALLATION

The original bolts that connected the transmission mount to the K-member were drilled for cotter pins and were held in place with castellated nuts. They're probably not as necessary as they were on 1930s-era streets and roads, but it's an OK and fun thing to do if you have the inclination and the hardware. We used reproduction hardware from Joe Nacewickz and added flat washers and cut lock washers before lining up everything and installing the cotter pins. Trust us; it won't come apart until you want it to, and it looks great!

Chapter 8

BODY AND PAINT

1928–1929 FORD METAL—THE BODY BEAUTIFUL

With the full-range of body pieces available from Brookville, plus complete new reproduction bodies, it's as easy to build a perfect steel 1928–29 roadster today as it was in the 1950s.

The 1928–1929 Model A roadster body is one of hot-rodding's all-time favorites. Whether platformed with its own original bones or sitting atop a Deuce chassis, it's one of Joe Galamb's nicest styling efforts, and we can't help wondering if when Ford's chief body designer penned this little honey he even imagined it would be so enduring and so cherished by several generations of hot-rodders. We wonder, too, what Joe might have thought of the substitution of the handsome 1932 radiator shell for the A's nickel-plated horseshoe. We'd guess that he would approve; the two were made for each other.

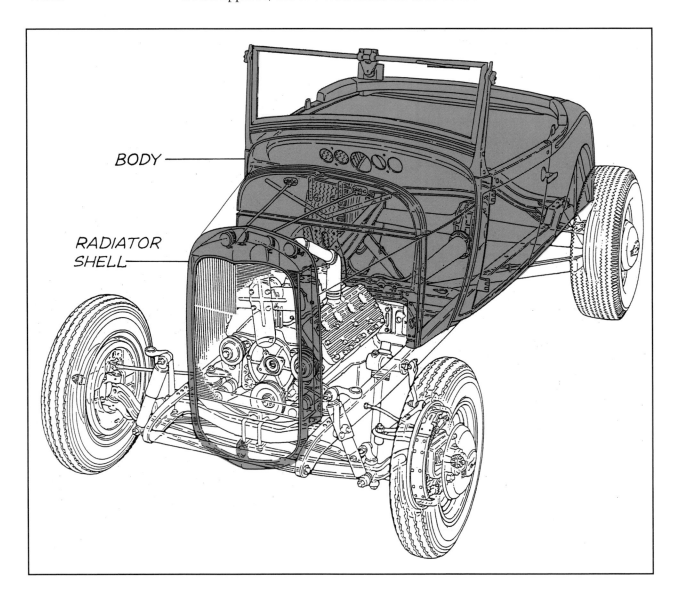

BODY

RADIATOR SHELL

We could probably get into some sort of aesthetic analysis of line, form, and proportions, and such to explain why the 1928–1929 roadster body is so popular, but we prefer to think that it's really because it looks great! Which amounts to the same thing.

Nice original bodies like this 20-year-old amateur restoration are rare—and pricey. This one would fetch about six thou'. The repaint along with original color and primer were removed with media blast process.

Original stretch lines on the firewall indicate that old Ford bodies are not nearly so perfect as we remember them to be. Damage was limited to a few extra holes in the firewall and some minor rust perforation in the rockers in the rear quarters.

To make sure the body looks as good as it's supposed to look usually requires some massaging, with the degree of effort closely related to how far out of shape the body is. If you start with an old original you no doubt have a lot of work ahead of you—rust and dent repair, door and trunk alignment, windshield fitting—and it's all part of the process. But even with a new steel body from Brookville you'll have to rub on some of the pieces to get everything to fit perfectly, just as you would with a flawless original body. Things like trunk and cowl fit may need a little extra care, and door fit and alignment are done when the body is fitted to the frame.

A common observation about the Brookville body—we hesitate to call it a complaint—is that the upper portion of the rear quarters need some coaxing to make them perfect. This isn't unlike work required on original stampings before they left the Ford factory years ago. Nor was this type of work confined to Ford; all auto manufacturers have had to finesse stampings into shape over the years.

In defense of the good people at Brookville, the draw in the upper part of the rear quarters is quite deep and complex, and a little bit of expert metal finishing or a skim coat of filler will correct the contour.

We chose a new Brookville body for the B-T Highboy because of time and cost, and because the actual work involved would be more like it would have been in the 1950s, when good original bodies were readily available.

BODY CORRECTIONS

There's no possible way for us to address all the problems needing correction in original Model A bodies; with at least 69 years for them to get into mischief, there are probably as many problems as

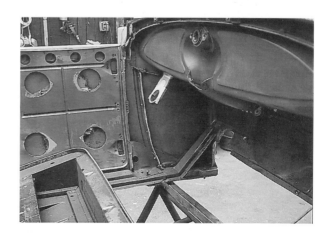

As good as the condition of this exceptional old body is, it's rough compared to a new steel 1929 from Brookville.

We added weld to the tops of the B-pillars and the edge of the doors on our Brookville body to improve the fit and sharpness.

The door top edge has been built up with weld and rough shaped. During the final fit it will be carefully matched to the fresh B-pillar edge.

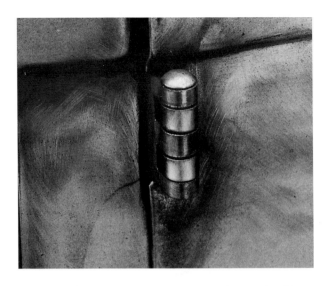

The door hinges were carefully massaged to work without binding, then filed to a neat cylindrical shape when closed. A chamfer was filed around the edge of each separation to minimize paint chipping when the doors are opened.

The rear body corners should be matched to the contour of the cross rail, and the separation line made the same width as it is across the back of the body.

there are surviving bodies. If you're using an original body you'll have to assess its condition and proceed accordingly. Suffice to say that an original body should be bolted to its stock frame before any serious work is attempted. A true Model A frame in good condition makes a great body jig, particularly if it's the frame that will be part of the final car.

We can take a look at some specific areas that may need correcting in a typical Brookville body, however, based on observations and first-hand accounts. Keep in mind, we're not correcting flaws so much as we are doing an acceptable amount of "fine tuning" on the reproduction body, very much like the essential work that was done in Ford's factory body shops in the past.

The door and post fit may need tailoring to square the top of the rear latch-post corner with the rear edge of the door cap. Since this is an area that's likely to receive some knocks, any buildup that's required should be done with weld rather than filler materials. And be sure to leave at least 1/8-inch clearance between the door and the post to allow for the natural flexing of the body.

The door hinges can also stand some attention to shape them up and to minimize chipping the paint on them when the doors are opened and closed. After the contact areas on both hinge halves have been sanded or filed flat, the hinges should be reassembled and sanded or filed to form a neat cylinder, with the hinge in the closed position. Then, a chamfer should be filed on each separation line with a triangular-section Swiss file to remove sharp edges. This will permit the paint to feather and blend, and reduce the tendency for it to chip at the edges.

The lower rear corners of the body, where they meet the rear body cross rail, may need some rework to match them to the rail. Most of this area can be hammered and dollied into shape, and it may be necessary to remove the rear body panel to reach inside the corners. A little metallic filler is OK in this area to fine-tune the shape.

The beltline reveal that extends down the rear quarter is indistinct on some bodies, but hand filing the creases can make it crisper. It may even be necessary to add metallic filler to the reveal beforehand and then shape it by filing or grinding.

Finally, the body needs little more than a good primer-surfacer in the finishing process to allow you to get rid of the normal waviness that occurs on stamped sheet metal panels.

It's fact, not fiction, that there were some near-perfect original Model A bodies produced in Ford plants 60-plus years ago, and you can bet that the best ones had the kind of help we've just described to reach their state of gracefulness.

The beltline reveal is sharpened by filing its edges. If necessary, add some metallic filler or lead to the reveal and file it to create a sharp, even line where it meets the flat area of the quarter panel.

The notch in the rail is boxed for strength and neatness. The box wall is a strip of new 18-gauge, gas-welded in place. When the task is finished, it's hard to tell that the body wasn't always this way.

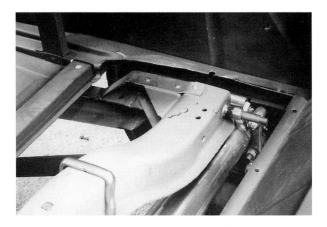

The rear body rails are notched to fit down over the rear cross-member after it's been stepped. We extended the notch, which begins at the rear of the last hat channel, back an additional 6 inches behind the cross-member to permit shock installation.

Covers to bridge the gaps between the rear floor pan and the body rails, created by the notch, are made from 18-gauge sheet with three breaks. The pieces are 18 inches long, 1 inch high and 2 inches wide, with 1/2-inch flanges.

BODY MODIFICATIONS

For a traditional full-effort A-V8, the rear of the frame is stepped to raise the rear cross-member, which in turn drops the rear of the body and the rest of the car to achieve the right stance. This means that the rear floor pan must be modified to make room for the intrusion of the rear cross-member, and while this sounds like lots of work, it's really pretty simple in this very modular body.

For example, if you're using an original body, first remove the rear floor pan from the trunk area. The panel is riveted in place. If you're ordering a new body from Brookville, it's even

We attached the side covers to the floor pan with sheet metal screws so they can be removed to make it easier to remove the pan from the trunk. The front of each cover is trimmed and formed to match up to the original rail.

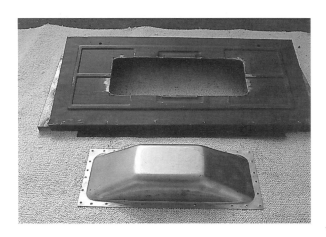

A hole was cut in the rear floor pan to accommodate a Model A sedan rear cross-member cover. This piece is spot welded into the floor pan, from the bottom.

less work, because that one is held in place with sheet metal screws.

The rear body rails must be notched to fit around the ends of the raised rear cross-member and then boxed to put the strength back in the rails. Simple covers that attach to each end of the floor pan to cover the new openings in the body rails are made from 18- or 20-gauge sheet metal.

You must also add a hump to the rear floor pan in the rumble seat-cushion area, to clear the top of the cross-member. In many early rods the rear floor pan was simply omitted, which eliminated this problem, but it sacrificed a lot of useable trunk space. You can fabricate a raised hump in the floor or do as we've done and use one from a Model A sedan floor. It's a great-looking piece that's available from several of the suppliers listed in Appendix A for around $30. Cut a hole in the

The new sedan hump looks right at home in its new roadster surroundings.

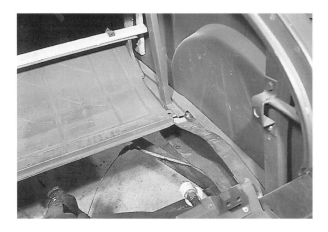

If you decide to use a Deuce frame for your A, the body rails must also be notched. Note that the rear vertical face of the hat channel has also been trimmed to prevent metal-to-metal contact between body and frame.

The rear trunk skirt inside the body must be notched for the rear cross-member, which sits farther to the rear with the 1932 spring-behind suspension.

Spruce body shims are made using the 1932 frame rails as templates. The horizontal cut along the bottom is made first, leaving the top edge flat. Then, the vertical cuts are made so the shim follows the frame contour.

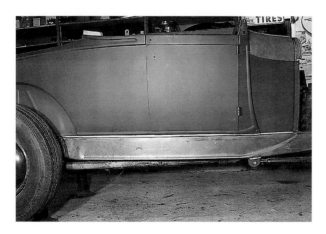

When the car is painted, the body shims will "disappear" (along with that unsightly gap found on a lot of Deuce-framed A-V8s).

floor pan, about 3/4 inch smaller than the flange on the hump, on all sides, and punch holes along the edge of the new hump. Then, spot weld the hump into the hole in the floor pan. Don't bother to seal the joint; there are no provisions for keeping rain water out of a Model A trunk, so you don't want to do anything to keep it in.

None of this work is particularly difficult or precise nor should it be. These bodies move around a bit and shouldn't be nailed down with close fit and boxing in areas where they are close to the frame.

For a 1932 frame, the body modification is similar, although the body side rails must be trimmed away a bit farther forward to sit down over the rising arc of the Deuce rails. If you're using a new body from Brookville, you can order it already modified to fit 1932 frame rails and save yourself a lot of work.

Radiator Shell
The Deuce radiator shell and grille are just about perfect as is, trim and all. It was common practice to fill the radiator neck opening in the top of the shell, however, particularly when the cowl was filled. For the cost of having an original shell filled, you can buy a new steel one from Brookville that is already "filled."

The lower edge of the sides of the shell must be trimmed about 1 3/4 inches to fit the shorter Model A radiator (see Chapter Five). Otherwise, the hood line will angle upward from the cowl forward, making the car look swaybacked.

The grille needs no modification, and if you're ordering a new one, make sure it has a crank hole; the work required to eliminate the hole on a stock-height grille wasn't worth the ef-

The hood flange on an original cowl gas tank is usually rather lumpy by this time, but it's easily corrected with some careful hammer-and-dolly work. This is a particularly critical visual area if you are planning to run without a hood.

fort then, nor is it now, and a Deuce grille without a crank hole is a relatively new street-rod manifestation.

Cowl and Dashboard

The cowl fuel tank was eliminated in most Model A-bodied hot rods, and the space was then used for instruments and electricals. The safest way to remove the tank from the cowl is to fill it with water and chisel it out around the edge. Cutting it out with a torch or even a high-speed abrasive grinder is an invitation to disaster because even thorough flushing of the tank won't necessarily eliminate lingering gas vapors.

The filler can be left in place, but the preferred look was a smooth, filled cowl. Brookville offers filled original cowls with the tank removed, or they will do the work required on your cowl if you choose.

Brookville also offers a blank 1932 dash fitted to the Model A cowl. It solves multiple problems by providing a mount for the steering column support as well as for instruments and switches, and it's a great and very desirable look.

A new steel 1932-style dashboard from Brookville solves several problems all at once. It lacks only the recess for the instrument panel to look like an original.

A badly butchered original Deuce dash was filled and mated directly to a 1929 dash cap to create this handsome custom dashboard in Bill Grainger's A-V8.

Firewall

When F-1/F-100 steering is used, the column passes under the bottom edge of the firewall, making the cutout for a stock Model A column unnecessary. It should be filled with a metal patch. Other than that, the stock A firewall needs no modifications.

Seat Frame

Moving the seat frame back a couple of inches yields more foot room in the tight Model A cockpit, room that is particularly welcome when getting in and out of the car.

With an original body, drill out the rivets that attach the seat frame to the floor, trim off 1 3/4 inches from the rear of the frame, move it back, and install it either with rivets or small bolts. If you're ordering a new body from Brookville, ask them to not install the seat frame. Then, trim and install it as just described.

Taillights

Taillights provide a great opportunity to individualize an A-V8, with lots of choices. Size and shape are the only limitations. For body-mounted lights, the mounting surface of the bezel should be flat or slightly curved to fit comfortably on the rear panel, and it should be no larger than about 6 inches in diameter or width or you risk overwhelming the rear of the body.

Self-contained lights, like the original Model A units or teardrop-bodied lights like those on 1937 Fords, were also popular and very practical. Mounted under the rear of the body on the cross rail, they leave the rear panel clean and uncluttered.

As a "styling" rule of thumb for surface-mounted lights, provide 1 1/2 inches to 2 inches between the light bezels and the edges of the panel to avoid a walleyed look.

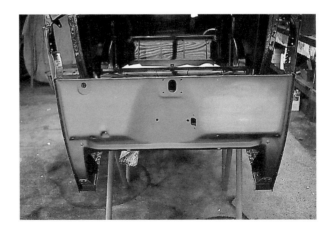

The lower left corner of the firewall in the B-T Highboy was filled to eliminate the steering column notch that's not required with the F-1 steering box.

These 1950 Pontiac taillights have been the premiere illuminator for the backside of A-V8 highboys ever since Don Ferrara installed them on his handsome red roadster 50 years ago. Thanks to Bob Drake, you can now buy a pair of perfect new ones (with glass lenses) for about the price of a pair of pitted and crazed swap meet lights.

There's no denying that Ford's most-popular taillight, the 1939 Ford teardrop, brightens up an A-V8 bustle just fine.

MOUNTING THE BODY

There's no rule that says when you have to mount the body on the frame—either before or after painting. But the quality of the paint and the ease of applying and finishing it both gain when the body is painted before installation. This way, the underside and insides can be finished as nice as the outside, and all the mess created during color sanding and buffing won't spread onto the chassis and motor. And while there's likelihood of a nick or three during installation, it's small potatoes compared to overspray and cleanup problems when the body is shot in place. Ya pays your money and ya takes your choice.

Setting the body on the chassis requires at least four healthy souls, one of whom is a take-charge sort and three who are good at listening and following directions.

But first, a little preparation . . .

Remove the steering wheel from the column and cover the column with a towel taped in place. Take the gear selector out of the transmission (and tape over the hole), and set the handbrake lever straight up and down.

Identify each of the wooden body blocks and its position, and cement the appropriate rubber pad to the bottom of each block with weatherstrip cement. Cement pads directly to the outboard cowl mounts on the frame. Don't set any of the blocks on the frame or stuff them into the body channels.

Close the doors and hold them in place with a bungee cord stretched between them; the body will flex enough that the latches will fail to keep the doors closed and they'll swing open and almost certainly be damaged—really!

Cover the rear cross-member with towels to prevent damage to the paint on it when the body is lowered into position.

If the trunk lid is installed, open and prop it so the lifters at the rear can steer the body safely over the cross-member.

Collect all the mounting bolts. There are eight hex-head bolts 3/8-16 x 2 1/2 inches and four carriage bolts 3/8-16 x 2 inches (for the outrigger cowl mounts on the outside of the frame). All mount points require upper and lower flat washers plus lower lock washers. (Omit upper flat washers from the carriage bolts.)

Talk your crew through the entire procedure—where to lift, how high, where to step, and what to watch for.

It's best to walk the body onto the chassis from the rear with the person at the left front in charge of the operation. As you get close to the correct position, visually line up a cowl mount hole in the body with one in the frame on one side; don't worry about the other side for now. Then, drop a body bolt in place, line up the holes on the opposite side and drop a bolt in place. Now, have the fellows in the rear slowly set the body down on the frame.

From beneath the car, set each body block in place while a couple of helpers carefully raise that side. The other helper drops a bolt in place as each block is positioned, then holds the bolt head while you add a flatwasher and run a nut on two or three turns. Do one complete side and then the other.

ADJUSTING THE BODY

Flexible old Ford bodies don't settle down until they're bolted to the frame, often requiring shims at strategic points to ensure that the doors will open and close on demand. Just as important, you'll want them to remain closed as the car travels over uneven streets and roads. Worst of all is pulling into your favorite drive-up eatery, with everyone watching, and having a door fly open without human intervention.

Before beginning, tape the upper corners of the doors and the door openings to protect the paint. Start securing the body by tightening the bolts at the rear, moving toward the front of the body. Skip the bolts in the outrigger mounts under the cowl and tighten the forward bolts, all the while checking to see if the doors will open and close.

Once all the bolts other than the outrigger bolts are tight and the doors open and close as they should, without chipping paint, and are lined up across the top edge, tighten the outrigger bolts and check door operation and alignment. If the adjustment changes as the bolts are tightened, loosen them and add rubber shims. This is a cut-and-try process and several shims may be required before alignment remains OK with the outrigger bolts tightened.

Billy Grainger's Magic Body-Adjustment Scheme

Body adjustment is much easier if the outrigger mounts are removed from the frame, the holes in the frame enlarged, and the mounts reattached with bolts.

During final adjustment and tightening of the mounting bolts, the outrigger mounts are left loose on the frame, the body bolts tightened with just a single shim, and then the outrigger bolts to the frame are tightened. It works perfectly.

PAINT—'TAINT WHAT IT USED TO BE

There's enough essential information about paint and painting to fill a book the size of this one, and there are some good ones available, particularly those from the paint manufacturers (see Appendix A). In this book we deal with specific guidelines, plus some "do's" and "don'ts" that we've found helpful.

Painting your hot rod used to be so easy. Once you were ready to step up from primer to gloss, all you needed to think about was color and how much. That it would be nitrocellulose lacquer was a foregone conclusion, and whether it would be 5, 10, or 20 coats was just a matter of money and time.

Looking back, with all the objectivity possible considering that it was probably one of the very best times in our lives, those old nitro jobs were almost as good as we remember them because there never was a paint better designed for impatient, inexperienced youngsters than nitrocellulose lacquer. You could shoot it in the driveway with a borrowed gun and a rented compressor, learning as

you went. You could correct your mistakes as soon as you made them, and the final finish just got better and better as you pumped more and more time into the process. Nitrocellulose lacquer thrived on attention. Of course, most of it wound up on the ground during color sanding, and that which stayed in place was prone to chip off in dime-size pieces, right down to the metal, but man! did it look great when it was fresh. And it was pretty easy to keep looking fresh because it was so easy to spot in and then repolish.

For most of us, nitrocellulose lacquer is little more than a fond memory today, legislated off the shelves in most parts of the country. And some of those wonderful acrylic substitutes are likewise contraband in the megalopolises of the East and West. This is because they're all full of VOCs—volatile organic compounds—which are the solvents that evaporate as the paint dries and cures. And since VOCs have been determined to be bad for the atmosphere, using less of them seems to be a good idea.

While a driveway paint job is a punishable offense for some of us, there are a lot of you who can shoot whatever you want, just as long as it doesn't rile your neighbors or the community constabulary. We won't even go into the social conscience thing here; if we were really responsible we'd tell you to send back this book, demand a refund, and stop spending your children's inheritance on yourself.

We will give you some important advice that may just keep you out of jail, at the very least, and make the painting side of your project fun on the positive side: Check with your local paint dealer or a field rep from one of the paint manufacturers like PPG or DuPont to learn what you can and cannot do, and ask them for any assistance they may want to extend. For these folks, car painting is life itself.

No matter where you live, your part in achieving a first-class paint job is limited only by the skills and facilities available to you. Even if you can go no farther than primer-surfacer just prior to color, you can do and control most of the work that will determine the quality of the final finish.

Being good neighbors and responsible inhabitants of Planet Earth, we have a strong preference for the new low-VOC paint systems, and we're particularly fond of the total systems from PPG and DuPont that begin with metal preparation and carry right through to final detailing of the gleaming finish.

Suede or Shine

There's no rule that says you have to go directly to glossy paint just because you can afford it. There are some pretty compelling reasons for running in primer for a while, if not forever. First, there's cost; a really good protective primer or primer-like finish costs as little as 20 percent of the cost of the shiny stuff in material alone. Second, it takes a fraction of the time to "finish" a rod in primer than it does in gloss, so you're on the road sooner. You can lop off a couple of hundred hours of project time that would be taken up with the creation of a perfect surface for paint. Third, and tied closely to the second reason, is that you can concentrate on sorting out your rod to make it better, instead of fretting about how needed changes are going to mar perfectly finished surfaces. Then, when it's as good as it can possibly be, for now, you can treat it to gloss. And finally, if none of those other reasons can persuade you to go suede, consider that it looks great on the right car. A well thought out, carefully executed rod in flatskin is like greatness at the threshold, ready for the final touch but confident enough to know that it's OK to stay this way for now.

There have been great advances made with primer in recent years, just as there have been with paint. You can have a first-rate primer job that will look good and provide protection for years. Best of all, when you're ready for gloss, that same primer is the necessary first step to a high-quality paint job. We're talking about catalyzed epoxy primer, of course, and specifically PPG's "DP" self-etching primer, currently available in six colors; white, black, gray, green, light blue, and red—a redder red than old red oxide. For some other hues than those that come right out of the can, DP primers can be tinted, but only with other DP primers and not with toner. For example, adding a bit of black DP to light-blue DP yields a wonderful dark blue, which is what we did for the B-T Highboy. Our reasoning was that since the car was going to be painted 1936 Ford Washington Blue, a comparable hue in the etching primer would provide good camouflage for rock chips, making them almost invisible from more than a few feet away. The resulting primer looked so good that the roadster would have stayed that way for a while if it hadn't been the subject of this book.

If the DP primers don't offer you enough color choices, you might consider PPG 2KTS primer. It's tintable up to about 30 percent with toner, so you can create just about any color you desire. 2KTS is catalyzed for good durability and holdout, but it must be shot over a DP primer base.

Incidentally, DP self-etching primer is not porous like old lacquer and enamel primers. Three coats of DP, all by itself, will provide as much as 10 years of rust protection, we're told.

Twenty-first Century Paint for a 1950s Hot Rod

Great paint starts with a great foundation, and it doesn't get any better than clean metal. If you're beginning with an old body, remove all the old paint, primer, and filler right down to the bone. You have several options:

Commercial immersion stripping is the costliest method and can cause paint problems later on if all the chemicals are not neutralized or baked out of all the nooks and crannies.

You can chemically strip the body yourself for $50 to $100 in stripper, protective gear, and clean-up supplies. Count on spending a weekend of your time with this method.

Do what a lot of pros are doing and have the old paint removed with media blasting—a sand-blast like process that uses a plastic medium to remove paint and primer all the way to the metal without disturbing or damaging the metal. Some media blast services can also selectively remove rust once the paint has been removed, for an additional charge. For a Model A roadster body, paint removal with this method runs about $200. This is our favorite. Check your Yellow Pages for this service.

If you're ordering a new body from Brookville, ask them to protect it with a light coat of water-diluted soluble oil rather than lacquer primer, which is not the best base for some of the present paint systems and could cause problems later. The soluble oil treatment will keep the metal from rusting while the body is in transit, and you can maintain similar protection until you're ready to paint it. Then, a thorough cleaning with wax-and-grease remover will get rid of the protective oil.

Prior to primer application, the body should be given an intense wash-prime with Metalprep and Scotch-Brite pads. The solution should not be allowed to dry on the surface but must be thoroughly flushed away along with any contamination it's loosened. Then, the surface must be thoroughly dried with lint- and grease-free towels and clean, dry air. The result is a perfectly clean metal foundation for application of catalyzed DP epoxy primer.

Catalyzed epoxy primer like PPG DP 50 LF provides an excellent base as well as protection of the freshly cleaned metal during body work or for as long as you care to leave it that way. Epoxy primer is applied in two coats—a light tack coat followed by a heavier coat—using a 1.3–1.5 nozzle. If the car will stay in primer for a long time, two full coats—in addition to the tack coat—are recommended.

The B-T frame was leveled with metallic filler following welding and grinding, then with body filler, and finished with primer-surfacer prior to color.

The doors, trunk lid, and body hardware are all primed separately off of the body.

Small pits and imperfections like this are leveled with plastic body filler prior to primer-surfacer. Corrections to this door/body seam were made with weld buildup and filing.

After the inside of the body has been painted, all openings, including the floor, are masked prior to exterior painting. This prevents dust on the inside of the body from being stirred up when the exterior is painted.

The body has been primed with 4 to 5 coats of primer surfacer. After it has been guide coated, it will be blocked flat.

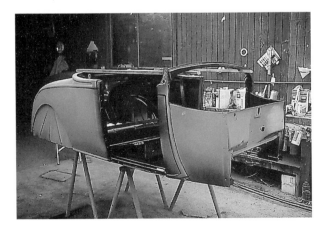

All door jambs and edges as well as the underside of the body are carefully painted at this stage to ensure good coverage.

The doors and trunk lid are installed prior to final painting to ensure uniform coverage with adjacent panels.

Play It Safe

For short-time exposure to primer, such as when spraying a couple of panels or individual parts, a fresh-air supply isn't necessary. A painter's mask and skin and eye protection are essential, however.

Don't even think about shooting catalyzed two-stage finishes without full protection and an appropriate fresh-air supply. In fact, don't even think about shooting this stuff at all; this is work you want to entrust to a pro who's trained and equipped to survive the experience. Unlike friendly old nitrocellulose, which would make you kind of goofy for a while and probably give you a monster headache, the new finishes can hurt you big time if you're not correctly protected. We're not lying, boys and girls.

Making Things Smooth

You already know what you have to do to bring the body up to snuff, so we're going to talk about making the hardware smooth.

Up first is the frame, and even if it's the very best Model A or Deuce frame you've ever seen it probably still has some surface problems. In fact, you introduced a few yourself when you filled unwanted holes and rearranged and added cross-members in Chapter Two.

Minor imperfections can be successfully covered with plastic body filler, but for really serious roughness, such as deep rust pebbling, we prefer to start with a skim coat of a good metalized filler like Alumalead or Metal-to-Metal filler. Applied over bare metal, it's the next best thing to weld— and a whole lot easier to work with, although a lot more stubborn than body filler.

Surface Preparation

Once bodywork is finished and the frame and suspension are smooth, you're ready to make the surface as perfect as you can—or care to—before final suede or gloss is applied.

There's no trick to achieving a perfect surface, just lots of careful, patient work blocking and reblocking the primer-surfacer once the metal work and panel alignment have been done.

The materials:

In addition to the catalyzed DP epoxy primer, you will need filler, such as 3M Premium Lightweight Body Filler, 3M Flowable Finishing Putty, and catalyzed primer-surfacer such as PPG NCP 271. You'll also need some contrasting lacquer and lacquer thinner for a guide coat.

The tools:

You'll need a 5-inch rubber block, a 10-inch long sanding board, a hand pad, and a cove block for negative curve areas.

Your sandpaper inventory should be equally varied. You'll need 40-grit to rough shape filler and 80-grit to final shape the filler and rough shape the putty. To final shape and feather putty, you'll need 180-grit, which is also used for initial blocking to flatten the surface. For blocking primer-surfacer, you'll need 320-, 400-, and 500-grit (for nonmetallic paint) or 600-grit (for metallic paint).

And you'll need protection, of course. A respirator is needed for working with the materials in liquid state, along with skin and eye protection when spraying primer. For blocking, a dust mask is essential.

For best results, primer-surfacer and paint should be shot with a 1.3 nozzle to reduce the grain of orange peel and reduce the tendency toward "urethane roll"—the characteristic waviness seen in many otherwise perfect current-tech paint jobs.

The technique:

The secret to correct blocking and sanding is to block and cross-block open areas in diagonal strokes, using light pressure, and allowing the paper to do the work. Diagonal blocking reduces the likelihood of cutting horizontal grooves in the surface

Applying filler:

Wet the surface with wax-and-grease remover to make it easier to see small dents and waves. Let it dry before sanding.

Scuff the area with 180-grit paper to give the surface some tooth for the filler to hold on to.

Apply a light coat of filler to the problem area. Be sure to wear skin and eye protection.

While the filler is still pliable and no longer tacky, shape it with 40-grit paper. Be careful not to remove too much filler or you'll have to apply a second coat.

Spray a thin contrasting guide coat over the filler, allow it to dry, and shape and feather it with 80-grit paper and light pressure. As sanding progresses, a guide coat indicates low spots where additional filler may be needed.

1 Color sanding begins with 1,000-grit wet-or-dry paper and progresses to 1,200-grit. A little dish soap is added to the water for lubrication.

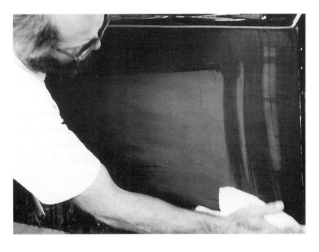

2 Water and sanding residue are frequently squeegeed off of the paint so the progress can be checked. This also helps get rid of tiny bits of grit that could cause scratches.

Applying Putty:

A thin skim coat of flowable putty over the filler fills sanding scratches and pinholes. It must be allowed to harden for at least a half hour.

Shape the putty coat with 80-grit paper, taking care not to overcut it.

Finish and feather the putty with 180-grit to avoid shredding the edges.

Applying primer-surfacer:

Primer-surfacer provides corrosion protec-

3 Contrast the uniform flat texture of the color-sanded quarter panel with the beltline reveal, which is untouched. When the panel looks like this, it's ready for polishing.

4 High points like these character lines on each side of the trunk opening should be protected with tape prior to color sanding and polishing. Paint tends to flow off of ridges and is relatively thin in these areas.

tion and takes the place of a second coat of DP primer where breakthrough is all the way to the metal. Before applying it, clean the entire area to be primed with wax-and-grease remover.

Start with a medium coat, followed by four or five wet coats.

Spray a thin contrasting guide coat on the primered area in preparation for blocking.

Begin blocking with a board and 180-grit paper to level the large areas and, as much as possible, move the board in diagonal strokes.

Use a sanding block for tight areas, with the same grit. For tight, negative areas, use a cove block to ensure smooth transitions and prevent gouges.

When 180-grit blocking is finished, reprime with two or three even coats, guide coat it, and block the area with 320-grit paper and water to get rid of orange peel and small imperfections. During this work, use a squeegee to remove water and loose material from the surface so you can check it for flatness. Your goal is to completely remove the guide coat.

Guide coat the panel once more and wet sand it with 400-grit paper.

Final block the surface with 500-grit (600-grit if the color will be metallic) on a hand pad to remove the 400-grit scratches. In this final step, block with continually random motions to prevent a pattern from forming on the surface. Don't forget to edge sand doors and door jambs as well as the trunk and trunk opening.

Applying Color

As great as suede primer is, there's something very special about a traditional hot rod with a killer paint job—although it would have been referred to as "sleek" or "snappy," which were equivalent expressions almost five decades ago. Perfect paint is the payoff, the reward for hour upon hour of hard, tedious work, both before and after the color is laid down.

Perfect paint today also requires some expensive facilities and equipment in many parts of the country. If you're in an affected area we recommend that you farm out the actual spraying to a pro and then do your own finish work—color sanding and polishing.

We also recommend that you opt for one of the modern paint systems like PPG's Concept. It will probably outlast you and require little more than a wipe or a wash and an occasional light waxing to keep it looking like it was just done. If you have your heart set on nitrocellulose and you can get away with it, Godspeed. It'll look great, traditionally handsome, and be in traditional need of frequent repolishing.

All of the work we've covered to this point will accept most earlier paints like lacquers and enamels and even wonderful old nitrocellulose, but it won't make them any more durable or care-free.

As we advised earlier, check with your paint dealer for rules and regulations about what you can and cannot do in your area. And make certain that any work you do is done safely with appropriate protection for eyes, skin, and respiratory system. Catalyst-activated, low-VOC paints are hazardous to humans and animals when the products are in liquid or dry-dust forms.

Clean, uncontaminated surfaces and materials are essential to the perfect-paint process, from beginning to end. When you reach the color stage the rules get tougher. Not only should the air be clean and dry, the work area should also be kept clean, and all materials—primer, sealer, paint, clearcoat—should be strained.

The order in which things are done also directly affects the quality of the final paint.

Inside body color should be shot after all body and surface work has been completed, just prior to application of exterior color. In this way, the interior color traps dust and prevents it from being stirred up when the outside of the body is being painted. Also, all openings in the body—trunk, cockpit, floor—should be masked to seal the interior after it's been painted as extra insurance against stirring up any dust not held down by the interior paint.

Every piece should be cleaned with wax-and-grease remover before it goes into the spray booth, and then again after it's suspended or positioned for painting to remove any oil from hand prints. All surfaces should be wiped with a tack cloth and chased with clean air.

Color base coats should be applied 10 to 15 minutes apart using a 1.3 nozzle to ensure a fine orange-peel pattern. For a normal two-step finish, three coats are sufficient, but if the color is to be color sanded before application of clear, five or six coats should be applied to make sure there's enough material on the surface.

Clearcoat should be applied in five coats, beginning with a medium-wet first coat and then followed at 15- to 20-minute intervals with the subsequent four coats. Again, the nozzle should be a 1.3 to maintain a fine orange-peel pattern and minimize "urethane roll."

Color Sanding

Color sanding, to eliminate the orange-peel pattern and get the surface flat, should also follow a specific sequence.

Color sanding begins with 1,000-grit wet-or-dry paper on a 5-inch firm rubber pad and water with a splash of dish soap in the bucket. Some pros start with 600-grit and then change to 1,000-grit on the block, but this is risky for the inexperienced, because the 600 removes material very quickly.

Water and residue must be squeegeed off of the panel often so you can check your progress and make sure you're removing no more material than necessary to achieve a uniform, flat surface on the paint.

Final color sanding, with a hand-sanding pad and 1,200-grit wet-or-dry paper and soapy water, removes 1,000-grit scratches and gets the surface ready for polishing.

Polishing

Polishing, too, has its own hierarchy of steps and set of rules for a successful finish.

Polishing begins with a white fiber pad and 3M Perfect-It II Rubbing Compound. Light pressure, with only the weight of the buffer, smooth, steady motion across the surface, and frequent cleaning of the pad ensure that most of the shine will be brought up at this stage. Don't count on this being a one-pass job; it will probably take three or four polishings to get rid of all of the 1,200-grit scratches.

And when those scratches are gone, you're ready for some serious shine—the final buffing with Finesse-It II Finishing Material and a yellow fiber polishing pad.

A final machine glaze with a foam polishing pad and Perfect-It Polishing Pad Glaze increases luster and depth and adds some protection to the surface.

The final step in the perfect finish is hand-glazing with Perfect-It Hand Glaze applied with grease-free Wax & Glaze Wipes. Of all the steps leading up to this final glazing of a perfect finish, this is the only one you'll repeat on a regular basis.

BUYING PAINT SERVICES

While the increasingly more stringent rules and regs affecting automotive paint have inadvertently contributed to the development of last-a-lifetime finishes, they've also made it so tough to apply these wunderkolors that most hobbyists have been left in the lurch. As you can see from just our summary discussion of what's required, it takes a lot more time to ramp up to speed than most of us can afford. And there's the cost of all the equipment required.

Or maybe you'd just as soon have someone else do your prep and paint work. So, who's it going to be? Well, that depends on what you're after.

For a good quality finish on a car that's going to be a driver, a reputable production shop is probably your best bet. And if you're willing to step up for a first-rate, show-quality paint job, you want to have it done by a pro who does this level of work on a continuing basis. Just don't be surprised to learn that the cost may amount to 50 percent of your budget!

The next time you see a car with paint that's comparable to the quality you're after, ask the owner for the name of the painter. Then, visit the painter, tell him what you have in mind, and see if he's willing to work with you on progressive painting—all chassis parts shot separately, body brought in on a dolly. Some shops are OK with this kind of work, and others wouldn't do it no matter how much you paid.

Ask about time lines, progress payments if they agree to shoot things piecemeal, quality guarantees, and anything else that could affect your peace of mind throughout the project. Don't be shy. We're talking about some serious dollars even for a moderate quality job, and a competent pro shouldn't mind.

Check out the shop. It won't likely be spotless, but a good shop will be neat and free of clutter. Pay particular attention to the cars on hand. It's not unusual for some projects to get temporarily stalled, but if you see dusty old hulks that look like they've put down roots in valuable shop space, move on.

When you find a painter and reach the decision point, make certain the scope and details of the work are mutually agreed upon and documented.

Whether you do or buy, quality paint takes time. There's no magic involved. It just looks that way.

The results of roughly 300 hours of metal polishing, body corrections and metal finishing, filling, blocking, painting, color sanding, and polishing. And only about a third of the work requires a pro!

Chapter 9

CONTROLS AND INSTRUMENTS

Planning and locating the controls and instruments so they are convenient and comfortable enhances both driving enjoyment and safety.

MAKING THINGS FALL READILY TO HAND

Some of the hardest, most important work a hot rod builder deals with involves driver-vehicle interface—making the car steer, stop, and go, all the while keeping a wary eye on its vital signs.

One of the most important parts of this important work is making the interface comfortable, making it feel right. Modern designers, stylists, and engineers have a term for the interface: ergonomics. Thus, when it's said that a car is ergonomically sound or good it means that everything we push, pull, tug, or twist to make the car do what we want it to do is (A) located where it's

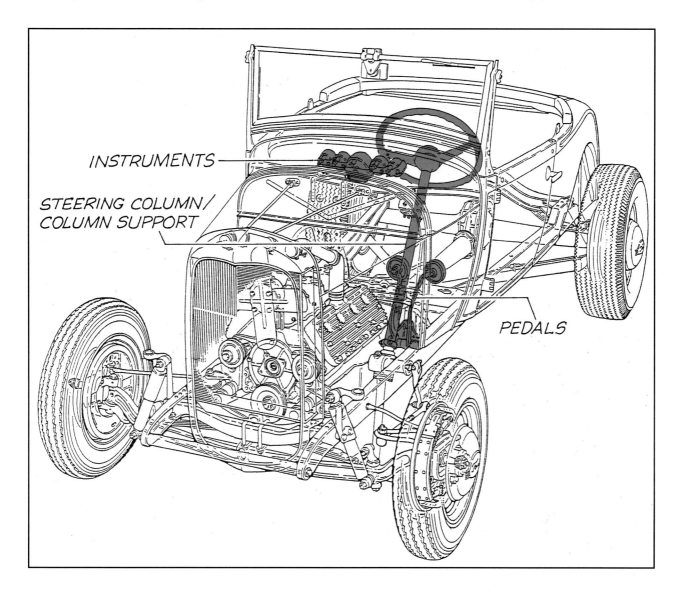

INSTRUMENTS

STEERING COLUMN/
COLUMN SUPPORT

PEDALS

supposed to be, (B) does what it's supposed to do, and (C) looks the way it's supposed to look for doing the thing it does. Old-timey sportycar journalists, working before ergonomics were codified, back when hot-rodders were building cars like the B-T Highboy, were fond of characterizing good ergonomics with phrases like "The gear selector falls readily to hand."

Labels and stilted language aside, the work is important and maybe not so tough—we hope—with the shared information we gained through some cut-and-try development of the controls for the Bishop-Tardel Highboy. This is probably the grayest of the gray areas in the early how-to magazine stories, and the reason that many highly reconfigured hot rods were a real handful underway. Most important, this is an opportunity to tailor your car to you, to make it your very own—ergonomically speaking. Think of it as "surprise-free" driving.

CONTROLS
With few exceptions, Ford hardware provided the material for control devices in the early and postwar hot rods. There was a surprising amount of as-is adaptability in spite of a couple of decades of models, and Ford hardware was some of the handsomest in the industry.

STEERING COLUMN AND COLUMN SUPPORT
We established the choice and adaptation of the steering box, a 1948–1952 F-1 unit, in Chapter Three, and now it's time to dress it up and put a wheel on it.

The choice of steering column is dictated by the steering wheel and the type of gearshift to be used. Early Ford steering wheels—Model A through 1939—sit atop a column mast jacket with a small flange just below the steering wheel hub. The ever-popular 1940 steering wheel sits on a larger bell-shaped cup. Appropriate aftermarket steering wheels, like the 3-spoke Bell and 4-spoke Cragar race car wheels, look best on top of the earlier mast jacket, although they look just fine with the 1940 jacket, so long as an adapter cap is used.

For top-shift transmissions in a car with a 1939 or earlier steering wheel, the early mast jacket is the obvious choice. With the 1940 passenger car or 1940-and-later truck steering wheel, a mast jacket from a truck with a floor-shift transmission is made-to-order for a top-shift transmission setup.

For a side-shift transmission you're locked into a mast jacket from a 1940 passenger car or 1940–1946 pickup. The modest bell at the top of this style mast jacket looks OK with pre–1940 banjo wheels or Bell or Cragar wheels, but it's

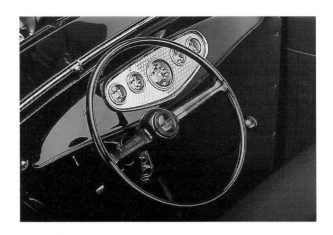

The 1940 steering wheel, also used in 1940–1946 pickups, is a classic handle for a postwar hot rod, in spite of being a little large for the Model A cockpit. A pickup mast jacket, without column shift, is used here.

The Bell midget steering wheel is more in scale with the small cockpit. A chrome-plated cap under the wheel blends with the large bell at the top of the 1940 mast jacket.

not as neat a pairing as it could be, and we're hard-pressed to recall a column-shift hot rod that didn't also include the very desirable 1940 steering wheel.

The column support is likewise dictated by the transmission shifter style. For a top shifter, any of the column supports from 1932 through 1939 are fair game, and the 1940–1946 supports are right for a column shifter. All Ford column supports, from 1932 through 1946, have an integral key-operated ignition switch and column lock. Retaining the column locking feature can turn into more work than it's worth, what with a shortened steering shaft and column, plus a relocated lock position. The convenient location of the ignition key and switch, however, makes a Ford column support an attractive proposition.

Ford banjo steering wheels have a fully contoured hub to match the top of the 1939 and earlier mast jacket with its small bell.

For the B-T Highboy, a small piecut was removed from the right side of this 1935–1937 column support. This allows it to match the curved lower edge of the Deuce dash and keep the lock level.

The mast jacket on the left is from a 1940–1946 pickup (without column shift), the one in the center is from a 1940 passenger car with column shift, and the one on the right is from 1939 and earlier.

The 1935–1937 column support we used in the B-T Highboy is a good example of what can be done. Designed for an essentially horizontal dashboard edge, we tailored it to the arc of the 1932 dash by removing a tiny piecut and rewelding it to fit, all the while keeping the lock cylinder horizontal. A small point perhaps, but it's just another one of those wonderful old details that keep all the disparate Ford parts looking like they belong together.

Steering wheel position, and consequently steering shaft length, is largely a matter of preference, with certain limits. The wheel should permit easy entry into the cockpit and be comfortably located. And it should look OK; an uncut shaft and mast jacket would ensure easy entry, and the resulting wheel placement would be all right in terms of control, but it would look pretty silly to have the steering wheel sitting up above the door tops.

Before you make any decisions—or nonreversible cuts in old Ford metal—bolt the steering box to the frame, bolt the body to the frame with blocks and shims in place, and bolt the dashboard in place. Then, position the steering column, column support, and steering wheel where you want them and then determine where to cut the mast jacket and where to position the column support. The rest of the work is a day at the beach.

PEDALS

The inclusion of 1932 pedals along with the 1932 cross-member was a simple solution to what could otherwise be a tough problem. Ford had already doped out the correct relationships of lever lengths and angles and fulcrums and force necessary to operate the clutch and placed everything conveniently close to the transmission. They'd also done most of the work for the brake pedal; all that remained was to relocate the slave arm to compress a hydraulic piston rather than tug on a mechanical rod.

The complete pedal assembly from the 1939 Ford was another favorite because it had the brake pedal all worked out and brought its own master cylinder along in the bargain. It just wasn't as easy to adapt as the 1932 assembly, although it's not uncommon to find 1932s that have 1939 pedals and master cylinder.

Our preference is for Deuce pedals, whether in a Model A-framed car with a 1932 cross-member or complete K-member, or in a 1932-framed car. It's much simpler to relocate the slave arm on the brake pedal assembly and fit a master cylinder on a custom bracket than it is to find a spot for a 1939 pedal assembly and then carve away at the left K-member leg until it fits.

Brake Pedal

For the brake pedal in the Bishop-Tardel Highboy,

The uncut, S-bend 1939 shifter is a thing of beauty and perfectly positioned and scaled for the A-V8 cockpit.

The complete 1932 pedal assembly bolts right into its original spot in the K-member, in spite of the K-member being whittled down to fit the Model A frame.

we cut the brake slave lever off of the top of the pedal base, chamfered it at 45 degrees on each side of the stub, and MIG welded it to the bottom of the base with successive passes on each side of the stub to form a strong new fillet all around the stub. The weld was then ground and polished to eliminate any fracture starters. With a Zerk fitting in a newly drilled and tapped hole next to the repositioned arm, the finished piece looks as if it had been made by Ford.

We also shortened the pedal arm itself by removing a 3/4-inch section so it would clear the bottom of the Model A firewall. Like the slave arm, the joint was made with a progressive buildup of MIG weld to chamfered ends, then ground and polished.

Clutch Pedal

Other than shortening the clutch pedal as we did with the brake pedal, nothing was required. It probably doesn't even realize that it's no longer in a '32 Ford!

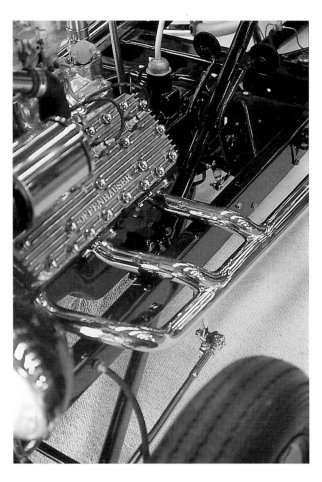

With the steering column in place and the pedal linkage connected, everything is just where it's supposed to be.

Throttle Pedal

The "spoon" throttle pedal assembly that was used on Ford cars and trucks from 1932 through 1938 is a hard part to improve upon. It's as simple and direct as can be, and with an integral return spring that could close big doors, it's hot rod perfect, even for the Model A firewall with its narrow four-banger cove.

We tailored a mid-1930s throttle pedal assembly to the B-T Highboy's Model A firewall by removing the spoon from one end, shortening the shaft and sleeve, and then putting it all back together again. Not only does it work great, but like so many of the other Ford-parts modifications, the pedal winds up looking as if it were always that way.

Repositioning the brake pedal slave arm from the top to the bottom of the sleeve permits the master cylinder to be placed behind the center cross-member.

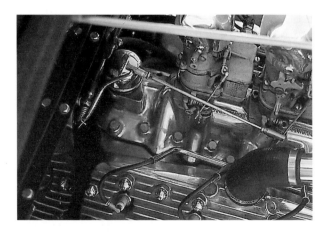

This mid–1930s throttle pedal was disassembled, narrowed, and put back together to fit in the narrow recess in the Model A firewall.

INSTRUMENTS

Instrument panels were given a great deal of thought and attention in postwar hot rods. That attention may well have come from the technical world of military service that many postwar hot-rodders had just left, although the relationship of high-performance and good instrumentation had been well established by the 1930s. Auburn, Cord, and Duesenberg cars of the day were instrumented to their teeth. An entire Auburn panel was a prewar and postwar hot button and one of the greatest pieces of work ever fit into a hot rod dashboard.

The old-Ford-correct satin finish on the throttle spoon adds to the car's authentic look. The adjustable throttle-foot rest is much appreciated on the highway. Think of it as vintage cruise control.

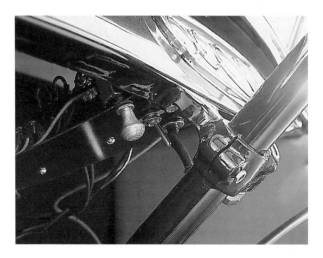

The starter button, electric fuel pump cutoff switch, and the headlight switch are located on the electrical bridge panel at the bottom of the dashboard, convenient but out of sight.

We "auditioned" a half-dozen instrument panel layouts from Haneline, including this Auburn-style cluster, which would have required extending the lower edge of the dashboard. Maybe next time.

The Haneline approach lets you see what looks good and what doesn't before spending a dime. For example, this eight-across panel, nice as it is, overwhelms the Deuce dashboard in the small Model A cockpit.

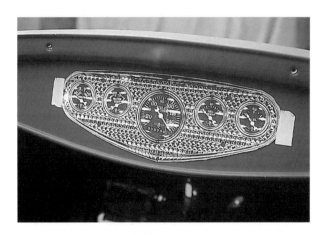

The pattern for the final choice, a Stewart-Warner Sports Panel, was centered on the dashboard, and hole positions were marked for the panel studs.

Instrument giant Stewart-Warner produced a line of packaged instrumentation set in handsome steel panels, often with engine-turned fascias, well into the 1950s. Often referred to as "boat panels" because of their widespread use in speedboats, the panels were popular with hot-rodders. The most popular of these was the Sports Panel—a five-gauge panel that looked like a

The panel, minus the engine-turned facia, was used as a template for marking the gauge holes on the dashboard.

stretched Deuce panel. The Sports Panel has remained popular for hot rod restorations as well as for nostalgia rod projects, and in recent years these panels shot way up in value. A couple of years ago, a hot rod hobbyist, who prefers to maintain a low profile, had the Sports Panel recreated in stainless steel so it would be available for the hot-rodder on a tight budget, just as the original ones were years ago. In combination with an engine-turned fascia from Haneline Products, king of the damascened panel, and Stewart-Warner's recreated wing-logo gauges, the new Sports Panel—which Haneline also markets—offers tradition-minded hot-rodders one of the best-ever dashboard looks at reasonable cost.

We chose just such a setup for the B-T Highboy, but not until we'd spent a few hours "trying on" different panel schemes to find one that met our instrumentation requirements and fit the 1932 dash panel whittled down and set into the Model A cowl.

We took advantage of Haneline's design service, in which they send you full-size photocopies of the panels you're interested in. This lets you decide which panel looks best, as well as make sure it will fit.

We started with several photocopies, including an Auburn panel, a straight-eight, a straight-six, and the straight-five Sports Panel. The Auburn and straight-eight panels overwhelmed the small Model A cockpit, and we were left to decide if we wanted a tach or not. Reasoning that tachs were uncommon on early flatmotor rods, we opted for the Sports Panel and a basic instrument kit that included a speedometer, water temperature gauge, oil pressure gauge, ammeter, and fuel-level gauge. As an alternative, a second water temperature gauge could be substituted for the fuel-level gauge, providing information on each cylinder bank individually—a common arrangement years ago.

When our panel arrived we first marked a vertical centerline on the dashboard to center the symmetrical panel.

We next transferred the stud positions from the actual panel to the pattern, then punched out the holes in the pattern and taped it to the dash, where we marked the stud hole locations with a prick punch. We then removed the pattern and drilled four holes, 1/16 inch larger than the studs so they could be easily fed into the panel.

Next, we marked the instrument holes on the dashboard, using the panel as a guide, removed the panel, and then cut the holes 3/16 inch oversize and deburred them on both sides of the panel.

After the instruments were trial fitted to the dashboard, the entire dash was installed in the body to make sure everything was OK before it was removed and painted front and back before final installation.

If you prefer a nonpanel dash, in which the instruments are set directly into the sheet metal, make full-size cutouts of photocopied instrument faces or discs of thin cardboard and tape them to the dashboard. Then you can determine instru-ment placement and numbers before drilling holes in your precious sheet metal.

Finally, there's nothing wrong with original 1932, 1933, and 1934 Ford panels and round-face instruments. The pieces tend to be a bit expensive, particularly for excellent panels and fully restored instruments, however. Just be sure the 6-volt instruments are ballasted if your car has a 12-volt system.

The instrument holes were cut 3/16-inch oversize with hole saws, then carefully deburred.

The instruments were installed for a trial fit, then removed while the dashboard was primed and painted both front and back. The Haneline/S-W system virtually ensures you will have a successful traditional instrument panel.

Chapter 10

FUEL SYSTEM

A good hot rod fuel system is much more than a manifold and collection of carburetors. Location of the fuel tank and pump, routing of the fuel lines, and throttle linkage "tuning" are key considerations for trouble-free driveability.

THE CLASSIC FLATMOTOR INTAKE

The classic intake for a street-driven hot rod flatmotor has always been a trio of Strombergs perched on a low manifold. In contrast, a pair of 97s had a half-hearted, almost sensible look, like maybe you used your rod for a morning paper route or delivered groceries after school. Four 97s—a full row of ducks—was strictly race stuff and even so, that much carburetion was reserved for really big motors and not something you were likely to see on the street, at least not for very long, or running well.

Yessir, three pots were right, serious looking, great top-end stuff, and livable—sort of. The stumbling and hesitation occurring at low engine speeds,

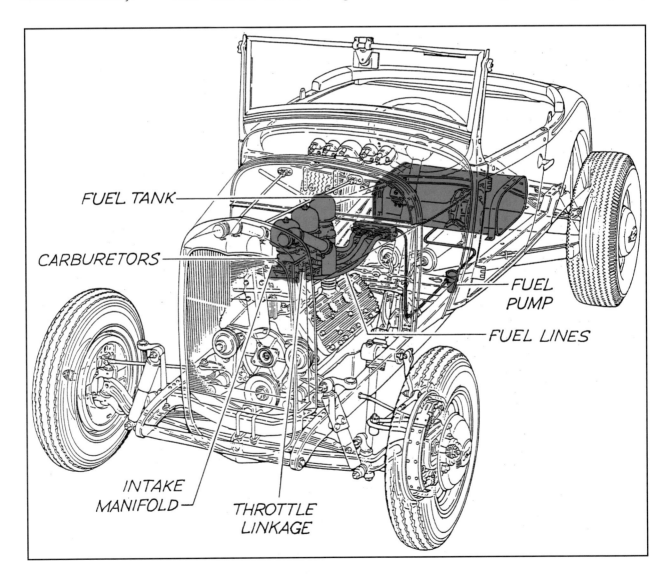

FUEL TANK

CARBURETORS

FUEL PUMP

FUEL LINES

INTAKE MANIFOLD

THROTTLE LINKAGE

thanks to the low airflow rate created by six venturis all opening at the same time, goes beyond annoying. But there is a way to have one's well-decorated cake and enjoy eating the admiring attention it gets at the same time. It's called progressive linkage and we'll talk about it later, after we deal with some other intake hardware fundamentals.

The best intake for a street motor is a two-carb setup with fresh Stromberg 97s—from a purely practical standpoint, the great look of three carbs notwithstanding. The airflow potential of three carburetors is just too much for the needs of small and moderate displacement flatheads at all engine speeds, so we know it's going to be terrible at low speed. The low airflow velocity at low and moderate engine speeds produces poor fuel siphoning through the jets, resulting in hesitation and flat spots during acceleration, a generally lean condition, and overall poor driveability.

Traditional "fixes" have proved less than successful. While the substitution of smaller Stromberg 81s for 97s sounds promising, the V-8-60 mixer isn't enough smaller than the full-size unit to make much of a difference. Changes in jets, emulsion tubes, accelerator pump stroke, and the like have little if any positive effect on the situation because they do nothing to alter the basic problem in a three-two system—too much air.

Before you get seriously involved in specing your system and purchasing pieces for it, we urge you to beg, borrow, or even purchase Tex Smith's *The Complete Ford Flathead V-8 Engine Manual* by Ron Ceridono. The carburetion chapter by Jere Jobe is worth the price of the book in that it will help you avoid the traditional mistakes that produce poor-running intake systems that can drive you nuts.

INTAKE MANIFOLD

Unlike old aluminum heads, old manifolds don't deteriorate and will last just about forever as long they aren't cracked or missing pieces around the mounting bolt holes. Stripped threads in the carburetor stud holes are fairly common, but they can be welded and retapped, and while this raises the cost of a swap-meet manifold, there are some, like the early Thickstun and Tattersfield high rises or an old Eddie Meyer or Edelbrock slingshot, that are worth the extra expense.

Offenhauser and Edelbrock are still producing new manifolds in two- and three-carburetor configurations, for both the early blocks as well as for the 8BA. They're also casting offset generator mounts, and Offy is even making their wonderful old fuel blocks again—if they ever stopped. These manifolds need virtually nothing other than port matching to your block and a shine if you like the bright stuff. A polished manifold is a lot easier to keep clean than an as-cast piece.

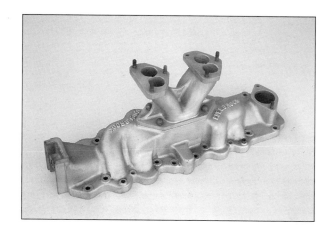

Prewar Edelbrock "slingshot" manifolds are plentiful and reasonably priced. It's a true 180-degree split-plenum design that works very well.

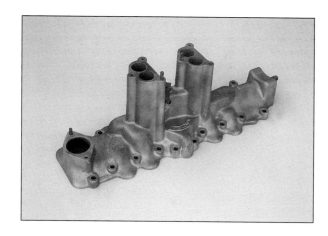

The second series Thickstun has excellent road manners. The tall risers eliminate generator clearance problems.

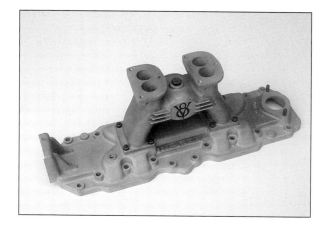

Bell Auto Parts dual is another prewar design that looks great and performs well. One as good as this might be a little pricey, however.

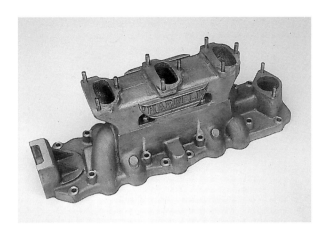

The Harrell triple is interesting looking and a rather good performer with its 180-degree dual-plenum design.

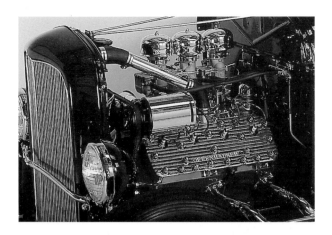

A trio of 97s in a row is pure postwar hot rod stuff. Carefully built and tuned carburetors, plus progressive linkage, provide great road manners as well as strong performance.

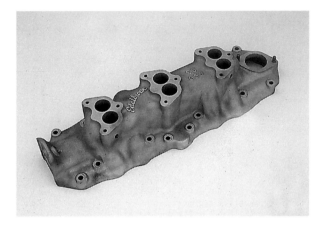

Postwar Edelbrock triple is easy to find at reasonable prices. In practical terms, for street applications, it performs as well as the latest versions.

CARBURETORS

The Stromberg 97 was and still is the most popular Ford hot rod carburetor for reasons as simple as the carburetor itself; it's flexible and forgiving and works extremely well when correctly serviced, set up, and tuned.

The Chandler-Groves, Holley, and Ford 94 types that replaced the Stromberg as the OEM carburetor from 1938 on can be made to work reasonably well on a built flathead, but they're more complicated and fussier than the 97. And while they had their fans, they received only a fraction of the time and attention paid to the 97—the odds on choice for a traditional hot-rod flatmotor.

The bottom-line objection to the 94-type carburetor is its vacuum-signaled power valve. The valve is designed to open and enrich the mixture to provide maximum power when it's needed. The signal to open comes from low man-ifold vacuum, such as occurs when the throttle butterflies are wide open, as they are during hard acceleration. As designed, for single-carburetor service on stock Ford and Mercury engines, the 94 was a decided improvement over the Stromberg 97, both in performance and fuel economy. The problem is that the power valve in the 94 is designed to enrich about 250 cid all by itself. So, if you add a second 94 you now have 500 cid worth of enrichment, and by the time we get to three deuces it's clear that it would take a modern "mountain motor" to handle the enrichment potential. In real terms, just two 94s provide far more enrichment than even a large displacement flathead needs or can handle. The result is gas-fouled plugs, particularly in small and moderate displacement motors. And while there are remedies, like plugs to replace the power valve, the complexity of the 94 makes it no friendlier to hot rods today than it was when it was new. We're sticking with the 97, just as the larger body of hot-rodders did long ago, because it's hard to argue against success. If you're still interested in the 94, read what expert Jere Jobe has to say about it in the Tex Smith book.

The Stromberg

The first thing anyone must have before even picking up a Stromberg carburetor is a Stromberg jet wrench. Even simple disassembly without this tool usually results in damage to the carburetor body and jets. You'll also need a float-level gauge during assembly, and both tools are available from Antique Auto Parts—also a great source of Stromberg bits and pieces, from jets, to rebuild kits, to complete reconditioned carburetors (see Appendix A).

3 The basic carburetor rebuild kit consists of all necessary gaskets and an accelerator pump. Be prepared to add a float-valve needle and seat and possibly idle air screws.

1 As old 97s go, this one is outwardly in good shape—no damage to the float-bowl top, no butchered screw heads, all linkage in place and in good condition. If it's as good inside, it's a keeper.

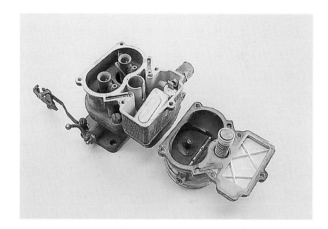

4 That old 97 looks just as good inside as it does on the outside. It's surprisingly clean and looks almost service-able as is.

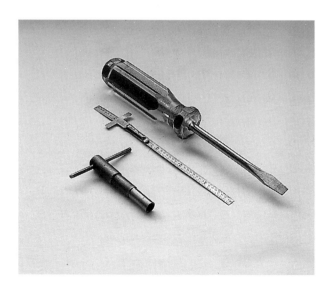

2 The basic Stromberg carburetor tool kit (jet wrench, float level gauge (or graduated steel scale), and screwdriver.

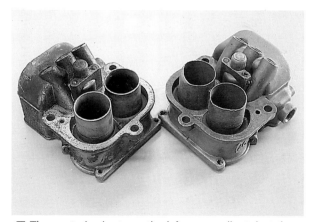

5 The venturi spigots on the left are excellent, but those on the right are probably too deformed to be coaxed back into shape.

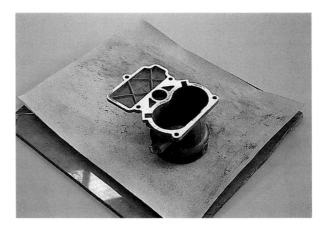

7 To help ensure a leak-free carburetor, the mating surfaces should be dressed with 400-grit paper on a super-flat surface, such as a pane of glass.

6 The size of a power valve is stamped on the flange. This No. 60—0.060 inch—is the leanest.

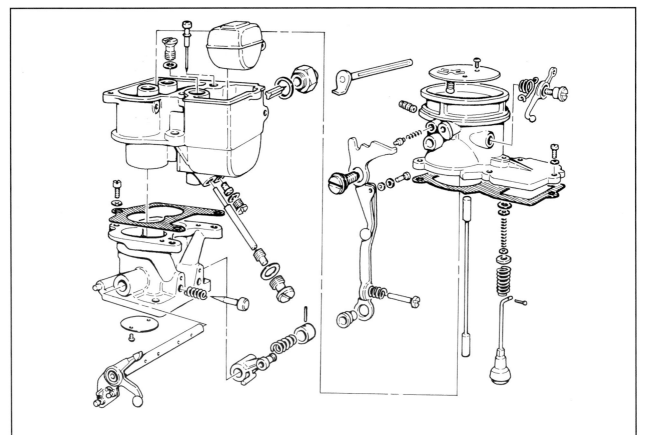

This diagram and the step-by-step assembly instructions and illustrations apply to both the Stromberg Model 97 and the Model 81/92 carburetors.

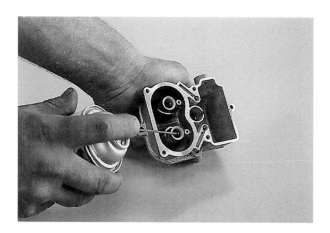

8 Following immersion cleaning, the passages should be cleaned once more with aerosol carburetor cleaner to remove any residue created during surfacing, along with any stubborn deposits not removed the first time.

9 Install the mainjets with the Stromberg wrench—just snug. Then install the cover plugs with new gaskets.

10 Adjust the float level using a Stromberg/Ford float gauge or a steel scale. The end of the top of the float should be 15/32 inch below the top edge of the bowl.

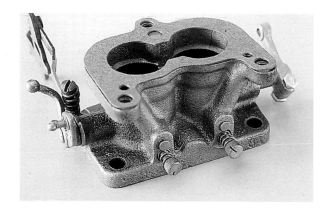

11 Carefully install the idle mixture screws and springs until they just make contact with their seats. Then back them out two turns.

12 Note the position of the return spring on the accelerator pump arm. Note, too, that the end of the arm is straight, ensuring full stroke.

What to Look For

First, make sure the carburetors you're buying are Stromberg 97s and not Chandler-Groves, Holley, or Ford 94 types. Most 97s have "97" cast on the left side of the body, although some are plain in this area. All Stromberg carburetors have a Stromberg patent number block on the right side of the float bowl, and the venturi size is cast on the right side of the body; most are 1 1/32 inch, and if you are buying 97s for a multiple carburetor setup, make sure they are all the same size. If the carburetor has a cast "81" or "92" on the body, it's a V-8-60 model, smaller than a 97, and not suitable in a mix-and-match arrangement; if you have two or three 81s or 92s, however, they'll work just fine together. Numbers aside, the Stromberg has external accelerator pump linkage, and the fuel inlet is plumbed directly into the side of the float bowl.

Look for overall good physical condition. There are a lot of good 97s still available, although many of them show signs of abuse. Make sure the carburetor has all its hardware, and check for external damage, like scars on the top of the float bowl where it's been hammered on to unstick the float. Cracks and chips in the body render a 97 scrap, because the body is not repairable, but you can replace a battered top. Damaged screw heads are often indicators of stripped threads in the body—again, unrepairable damage.

If possible, buy a good extra 97 for parts. A good way to buy 97s is as an old three-, four-, or six-two setup on a manifold for an early Olds or other overhead. These early fuel systems show up regularly at swap meets, have probably been sitting on a shelf for a decade or two, and at typical asking prices in the $200–$400 range are a bargain, plus you'll have spares and trading material.

Inspect the inside of the carburetor for condensation damage or electrolysis. The discharge nozzles and tubes should be in good condition, as well as the float, primary jets, and power valve. The condition of the accelerator pump is unimportant, because you'll be replacing it.

Separate the body from the base and check the ends of the venturis where they fit into the base. They should be round and smooth with no chips or cracks. They are easily damaged if the body has been dropped, resulting in leakage and poor performance. You can correct minor distortion by warming the body in the sun for about an hour (the metal is very soft) and then gently rolling the venturi back into shape with a socket.

Make sure the throttle shaft turns smoothly with little or no play, but don't pass up an otherwise excellent carburetor just because the throttle shaft is sloppy; the base can be rebushed, and new throttle shafts are available.

Check the power valve for size and operation. A No. 63 is good for street applications with duals, and the valve should operate freely. Larger valves—higher numbers—provide greater top-end power but hurt economy.

Check the size of the primary jets. Small jets are for gasoline, and large ones are for alcohol—not an uncommon find in an old 97 with an uncertain history.

Also check the main jets; they may have been drilled out. If you suspect that this may be the case, check the actual size with a number drill corresponding to the size stamped on the jet. If the jet orifices have been enlarged, don't use them because there's no reliable way to determine their true size or flow capacity. Orifice size is stamped on the flank of main jets and is a real-world dimension; a "45" jet measures 0.045 inch.

For a mild street motor with duals, No. 45 main jets work well for performance, driveability, and economy. For three 97s, start with No. 40 main jets and adjust as needed.

The sizes of the power valve, the primary jets, and the mainjets all affect carburetor performance and are easily changed; assume that they have been.

Finally, check the length of the accelerator pumps rods. There are two different length rods for the 97, and the longer one is for carburetors with two connectors on the bellcrank on the throttle shaft. The one nearest the shaft is for summer operation, and the other one is for winter, when a richer mixture is desired. On carburetors with this style bellcrank, the short rod won't depress the accelerator pump far enough to open the power valve, resulting in poor acceleration and top end performance, so you will need the longer rod.

Disassembly, Cleaning, and Corrections

The Stromberg is so simple there's no need for detailed disassembly instructions. Just refer to the exploded drawing as you take it apart and get acquainted with the pieces and how they fit together.

The parts are small enough to be easily cleaned in a small dip-basket carburetor cleaner can. Just be sure to follow the cleaner manufacturer's directions for immersion time and neutralizing, then dry the parts with compressed air and clean, lint-free rags. And be sure to work in a well-ventilated area and wear your eye protection!

First, you must dress and true the mating surfaces so the carburetor won't be a leaker. It's a simple fix that's often overlooked. Surface the underside of the top and the top of the body with 400-grit paper on a sheet of glass. To surface the bottom of the body, use 400-grit wrapped around a file to work around the air horns.

Next, clean all of the passages in the body and base with an aerosol carb-and-choke cleaner followed with compressed air. This gets rid of the residue created by the surfacing, as well as any crud the carb cleaner missed.

At this point you must decide what finish you want on the carburetors—natural, painted, iridited cadmium, or chrome. Even after thorough immersion cleaning, the old bodies and tops are likely to be stained and mottled. Wily old restorers use a number of schemes to return old carburetors to an as-new state, all of which seem to involve acid of one description or another and sound decidedly risky. Sand blasting is out although a superfine bead blast does a nice job with very little change to the surface finish. We opted for a gold-cast cad wash on ours, applied by a plating shop.

Install the carburetor bases on the manifold and carefully line up the throttle shafts so they're parallel. This will prevent binding during operation.

Assembly

With the exploded drawing to jog your memory, you're ready to put the Stromberg back together. Take care not to overtighten things; snug is just enough. Even the screws that hold the top to the body shouldn't be tightened to more than 10 inch-pounds—just a little more than what's required to flatten the No. 10 lockwashers under the screw heads.

Install the pump inlet check valve, the main jets, and the plugs in the bottom of the body, using new gaskets.

Install the primary jets and the power valve, and be sure to include a new gasket for the valve.

Install the needle, gasket, and seat in the side of the bowl. If the point of the needle shows even the slightest bit of ridging, replace it and the seat. You might consider stepping up to Grose Jets at

this point. When correctly installed, they virtually eliminate flooding caused by sticking floats. Many of the suppliers of old Ford parts carry them.

Install the float, and check and adjust the level by bending the tab that pushes against the needle valve. The correct tab on a Stromberg/Ford gauge is the one nearest the hole in the float gauge. If you don't have a gauge, adjust the float so the end of the top is 15/32 inch below the top of the bowl.

Before installing the accelerator pump, remove and stretch the springs, reinstall them, and lightly coat the pump piston with clean oil. Then, install it about halfway down in its bore.

Guide the accelerator pump through the hole in the top and install the top on the body with a new gasket. Tighten the screws snug—no more than 10 inch-pounds. Then install the pump arm and spring, engage the arm with the pump shaft, and lock it in place with a cotter pin.

Install the idle mixture screws and springs in the base. Carefully run them in by hand until they just make contact, then back them out two turns. This is a good starting point that will allow the engine to idle when it's first started.

If you are doing a multiple carb setup, assemble each of the bodies but don't install them on their bases just yet. Instead, read on.

Installation

Bolt the bases on the manifold, with new gaskets, and leave the nuts just loose enough so you can move the bases. Then, line up the throttle shafts parallel to one another and tighten the nuts. This helps ensure that the linkage won't bind and prevent the throttles from fully opening or closing. Also, it reduces wear on the throttle shafts and the shaft bores.

Now, before you install the bodies on the bases, install and adjust the linkage.

THROTTLE LINKAGE

In addition to having all the throttle shafts parallel, it's important that all the throttle butterflies are fully closed during initial linkage installation and adjustment to ensure good idle performance. Once the linkage is installed and the carburetors are assembled, it's difficult to detect a throttle that's slightly open when the others are closed—aside from poor, virtually unadjustable idle performance.

Two-carb Installation

Install the left-side arms and connector rod on the throttle shafts and adjust the rod so the arms are parallel to one another.

With the throttles fully closed, position the left-side arms forward at about 45 degrees and tighten the set screws or pinch bolts that lock the arms to the shafts. Then, pull back the throttle lever on the right side of the rear carburetor to make sure the throttles open all the way and that the left-side levers are about 45 degrees to the rear. It's important to have a significant angle between the rod and the arms at full throttle to prevent the linkage from going over center and jamming the throttles open.

Alignment for a three-carb setup is essentially the same as for two. Also, set the throttle arms at about 45 degrees forward with all the throttles fully closed.

Three-carb installation

For a three-deuce setup, progressive linkage is a must. You can get the Offenhauser type that's been around for ages from Patrick's and other sources, or a new somewhat high-tech arrangement from Flathead Jack.

At first we tried the more traditional Offy linkage for the B-T Highboy, and once we doped it out—there are no instructions with the linkage—it worked well. This linkage required periodic "tune-ups," however, because the pinch bolts would loosen and permit the arms to slip on the shafts. We then tried Jack's linkage and found that it stays put, once it's adjusted.

Progressive throttle linkage on three Strombergs changes the character of the classic setup, making it almost as good as a single-carburetor arrangement for driveability, with all the capacity needed for a strong-running, large-displacement motor at high engine speeds. The center carburetor is the primary carburetor in a correct three-two setup, and the only one with a working choke. There's no need to remove the chokes from the other two carburetors—some tuning pros say the carburetors flow better with the chokes in place—but they must be secured in the full-open position.

Begin by installing the long arm on the primary carburetor at an angle of about 45 degrees forward, with the throttle butterflies fully closed, and adjust it for full stroke when the accelerator pedal is depressed.

Install the medium and short throttle arms on the first and third carburetors, respectively, and adjust them parallel to each other, angled forward about 45 degrees. Make certain that both throttles are fully closed.

We found that a good progressive setting has the primary carburetor throttle opening about one-third, or about 30 degrees, before the butterflies in the secondary carburetors begin to open. With our setup, on an Offenhauser manifold, the distance from the movable stop on the primary shaft to the arm on the front carburetor is about 2 inches for the Offy linkage and about 2 1/2 inches for Jack's, and the spring is lightly compressed. This places the movable stop just over halfway back from the forward arm to the center arm. Not all three-carb manifolds are dimensionally the same, so the position of the movable stop may vary slightly.

You'll need to fine-tune and dial in the linkage for your car anyway, because the level of engine buildup (stock to full-race), gearing, and weight of the car all come into play. Just remember that the closer the movable stop is to the long arm on the center carburetor, and the more the spring is compressed, the quicker carbs number 1 and 3 will open.

As a final safety check, make certain the throttle arms are adjusted so there is a significant angle between each arm and its operating rod at full throttle opening to prevent the linkage from going over center and holding the throttles open when the pedal is released.

FINAL ASSEMBLY AND ADJUSTMENT

Now, you can install the bodies on the bases, connect the fuel lines, install the air cleaners, and fine tune your system.

After the engine is running, pay attention to spark plug color for mixture information, just as you would with any other engine. At idle and low speeds, the idle mixture screws have a big effect on mixture. Turning the air screws out richens the mixture, and turning them in will lean it.

From about 20 to 70 miles per hour, mixture is controlled by the main jets. There are seven jet sizes readily available—two richer than our baseline 0.045 main and four that are leaner. At the top end of the scale, the power valve comes into play, and here there are five available, with 0.063 the leanest of the group.

Fuel Pump

There's really nothing wrong with a stock fuel pump for a street-driven hot rod, just as long as the pump is in good condition and the engine is fitted with the correct fuel-pump pushrod. With variations in the height of the fuel pump base from one aftermarket manifold to another, incorrect pushrod length is a common cause of fuel-feed problems.

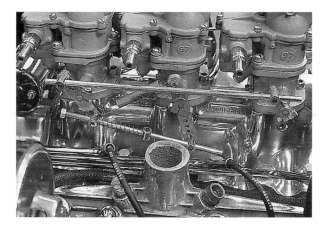

This Offenhauser progressive linkage is very much like the linkage from Flathead Jack in design and operation, just not quite as precisely manufactured.

The pedal-to-carburetor linkage connects to the center carburetor on a three-pot setup. With a pair of 97s, connect the link to the front carburetor.

One of the easiest problem-solvers, then and now, is eliminating the stock pump and adding an electric pump to the system. We opted for the easy way out and mounted an Autopulse electric fuel pump on the center cross-member. This is essentially the same pump that's been around since the 1940s—still available, although now it's called a WALBRO WEP-38. This pump is well suited to the Stromberg carburetor in that it produces no more than about 3–4 psi pressure; modern 6–14 psi pumps overpower the needle valve and force fuel down the venturis and out through the "vent" where the accelerator pump plunger passes through the bowl cover. And be sure the pump you buy is rated for your electrical system's voltage. The part number for this pump is 12V2403 and it sells for around $75.

Fuel Tank

Fuel tank location has always been a small problem in Model A highboy hot rods. Almost invariably it was solved by putting the tank in the trunk because, as it turns out, that's the best place for it.

A popular traditional solution was to use an elliptical 1920–1925 Model T tank mounted in the rumble seat footwell behind the Model A's seat. We're pleased to tell you that this is still viable today, thanks to the restoration hobby. Brand new Model T fuel tanks and mounting brackets sell for about $125 to $150 and not only do they look right, they're galvanized and baffled and just as neat as can be. Add a polished Ford-script gas cap and a Stewart-Warner fuel sender to the tank, and it just doesn't get any better.

Fuel Lines

Steel and neoprene are the only two materials suitable for fuel lines in a traditional hot rod. You know, of course, that copper line is an invitation to a car fire because it rapidly becomes brittle and fractures. And of course braided flexible lines, no matter how good and handsome they are, have no place back in time.

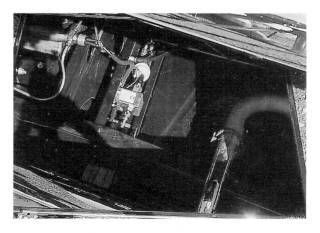

An electric fuel pump and filter should be installed out of harm's way but accessible without major disassembly. The hard line from the tank to the filter is mounted on standoffs and connects at each end with a short length of fuel-service Neoprene hose and spring clamps.

The hard lines in the B-T Highboy are 5/16-inch steel tubing made up in two sections—one from the tank to the filter and pump, and one from the pump to the firewall. Short sections of fuel-service neoprene hose are used for the connections and are held in place with spring clamps.

The firewall hard line connects to a fuel block that feeds three 5/16-inch fuel-service neoprene hoses that connect to the carburetors. Here, too, the hoses are retained with spring clamps.

Air Filters

If you're using new louvered or helmet-style air cleaners, check the filter elements to make sure they are for automotive service. Many of the new elements we've seen recently are much too dense, intended for air-compressor duty, where the airflow rate is much lower than that required for an automobile engine. The suspect filters contain 120-plus folds, whereas an equivalent automotive filter will have 50 to 60 folds.

The "compressor" filter creates serious mixture problems that can't be simply tuned away.

The B-T Highboy started life with these filters, and while it ran OK, it was much too rich, and fuel consumption was high. A change to correct filters, from NAPA, leaned out the mixture and boosted fuel economy by 50 to 60 percent!

On close examination, most remembrances involving the hot rods of our youth contain a fuel leak or two, perpetually stuck floats, and driveability gremlins that just wouldn't go away, no matter what we did.

But we know that doesn't have to be so today. There's still lots of good information available—maybe even better information because there's so much more collective experience with the hardware than there was in the 1940s and 1950s. And all of the right stuff from then is available now—plus some things that didn't exist, like Grose Jets and brand new fuel tanks and neoprene hose that doesn't get brittle or rot away in a few months.

Years from now, when we look back on the old-Ford hot rods we build today, they really will have been as good as we remember them.

A new 1920–1925 Model T fuel tank is perfect for a traditional A-V8 roadster. By offsetting the 10-gallon tank to the left in the trunk, there's ample room left for a battery box.

Chapter 11

ELECTRICAL

A 6-VOLT SYSTEM IN A 12-VOLT WORLD

With 12 volts on tap and modern vinyl-insulated wire protected with reproduction early harness covering, the electrical system is functionally up to date but traditional in appearance.

Way back in the 6-volt 1950s, the best way to confirm if some stranger had a really baaad motor, without actually risking next week's gas money and maybe breaking some parts in your own car in the process, was to listen when he started it at the roll-up eatery after a half-hour pause for a burger and Coke. If the motor spun easily with that wonderful "rrr-rrr-rrr" Ford starter sound, it was a pretender and the guy probably had the choke about half closed to make the motor lope when he pulled in.

But if that first compressing cylinder almost stopped dead before the motor burst to life with a wondrous roar, this was a rod to avoid unless you were

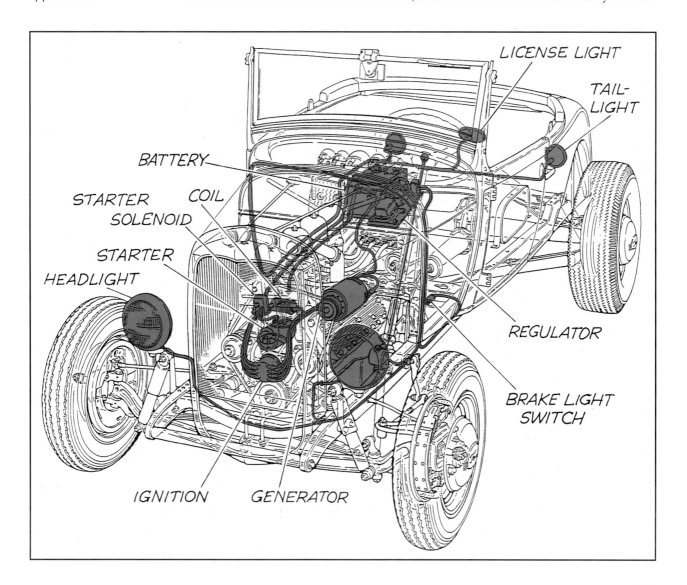

Converting a 6-volt generator to 12-volt operation is done simply by replacing the field coils in the generator case. It's also a good idea to replace the front bearing and seal and the Oilite bushing in the rear cover.

An original-style wire cover neatly disguises modern wiring. The cover is available in 1/2-inch, 7/16-inch, and 3/8-inch diameters.

running something equally as nasty under your hood. Such was the tale of a scant six volts of stored electrical energy used to crank a high-compression flathead.

While a 12-volt system may seem a little out of character with a postwar hot rod, the elements required for the upgrade—generator field coils, regulator, ignition coil, bulbs—existed at the time, so the job was doable then and within the constraints of creating a pure old-tech car today.

GENERATOR AND REGULATOR
Converting a 6-volt Ford generator to 12-volt service requires little more than replacing the 6-volt field coils with 12-volt windings. And while you're at it, replace bad bearings and brushes and give the armature a bright shine with crocus cloth.

When installing the field coils, make sure the hot coil isn't grounded in the case; there's an insulating washer on the inside as well as outside.

New generator parts, including 12-volt field coils and a 12-volt regulator, are available from several of the suppliers listed in Appendix A, so check your catalogs.

Finally, don't forget to lube the oilite bushing in the rear cover with a few drops of motor oil when you assemble the generator. Then, each time you check the engine oil level, drip a couple of drops from the dipstick into the oiler on the rear cover.

STARTER
Nothing need be done to the starter, as long as it's in good condition. It's quite happy with a 12-volt jolt and will spin a flathead to life almost before you can release the starter button.

LIGHTS AND SUCH
All of the devices for a 12-volt system must be rated for 12-volt service—bulbs, switches, circuit breakers, fuses, relays, as well as the ignition coil.

WIRING
Accurate, period-perfect restoration-quality wiring is readily available for old Fords, but the looms require modification to delete unneeded wires and add some not originally included. We recommend a more straight-forward and less-expensive approach using modern vinyl-insulated automotive wiring sheathed in impregnated cloth loom cover. Not only does this give the wiring a traditional look, it also camouflages it. The wiring on the B-T Highboy all but disappears against the dark Washington Blue paint. The wiring cover is available from several of the old Ford parts suppliers in Appendix A. We recommend you purchase 10 feet each of 1/2-inch, 7/16-inch, and 3/8-inch, along with 30 feet of 1/4-inch cover. Each size cover fits nicely over the next smaller size, making it easy to produce really handsome, graduated looms.

THE SYSTEM—TYING IT ALL TOGETHER
There's not much wiring nor many electrical devices in a car this small and simple. Still, preplanning is essential for a successful system. Working with ace wireman Terry Griffith—who has wired perhaps half the hot rods in northern California—we opted to hide the devices that are normally screwed to the firewall, things like the voltage regulator, ignition ballast, fuse panel, and solenoid. We mounted all of these, except the solenoid, under the cowl on a bridge that runs from the dashboard to the firewall. The

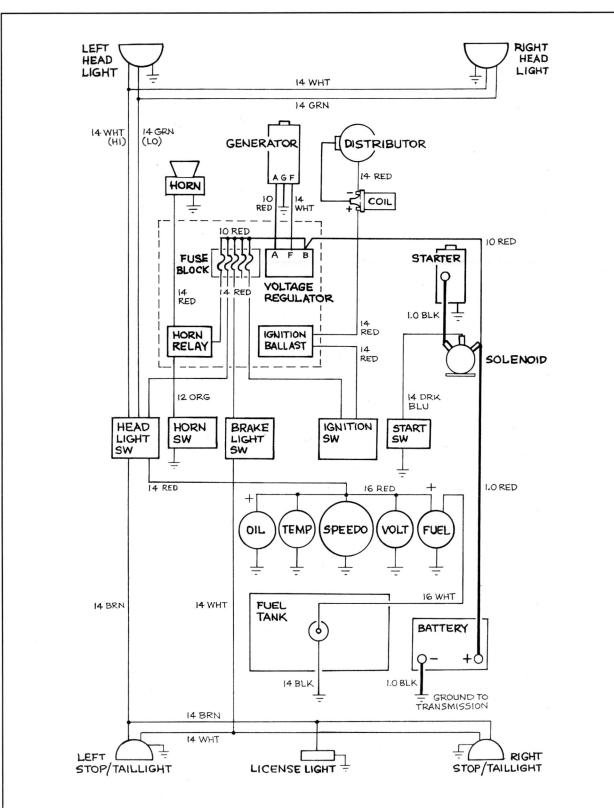

The wiring scheme is as simple and straightforward as the rest of the hot rod. We find it helps the actual wiring task to color code this diagram with colored pens or highlighters beforehand. And, if you use a different color of wire at any point, be sure to note it here so you'll have a permanent record of your car's wiring scheme.

The electrical panel attaches to the firewall and the bottom of the dashboard. It mounts the voltage regulator, horn relay, ignition ballast, switches, and the vertical fuse panel.

starter, headlight, and fuel-pump cutoff switches are also installed on the bridge, out of sight but easily reached by the driver.

We mounted the fuse panel on edge with an angle bracket on top of the bridge, with the fuses facing the right side of the cockpit so they're easy to see and identify by looking up at the panel from the passenger side. We had considered some neat tricks like a hinged swing-down panel and even thought of mounting the fuses under the bridge facing down, but either remedy would have created wiring problems. This one is just good hot-rod-simple thinking.

We made the bridge from 16-gauge steel to give it some strength without the need of ribs or folded edges, reasoning that it's not a good idea to place stiff "fulcrums" in flexible Ford bodies.

The solenoid was mounted on a simple bracket that's held in place by the right front body mount bolt. The solenoid is close to the starter, out of sight, and still accessible from the engine compartment.

The wiring diagram is for a very simple system. We've eliminated a headlight dimmer switch, using instead the two positions in the main switch for high- and low-beam circuits. We have included a high-beam indicator lamp, however. There's an unused position on a six-fuse panel for a radio or maybe a heated vest, and as

sparse as the system is, it's legal anywhere we'd want to drive.

We've also included the routing scheme we used for the looms in the phantom view at the beginning of this section because this is almost as hard to dope out as the wiring itself. We also got Terry to offer some simple guidelines for wiring:

- Start wiring at the device and work toward the power source or control. For example, start at the left headlight, using 1/4-inch cover. Then, do the right headlight in the same way, but when the four wires come together, switch to 3/8-inch cover. This is also the point to introduce the single horn wire coming out of the bottom of the steering box. And be sure to cover that wire with 1/4-inch cover.
- To bring an individual wire out of a loom to connect it to a device, cut a small slit in the cover a half-inch from the connection point. If the wire is more than 1 inch long, it should be covered with a piece of 1/4-inch cover.
- Loom cover junctions should be taped with a neat wrap of plastic electrical tape. Don't overdo it; one or two wraps is sufficient.

BATTERY

The battery is mounted in the trunk, at the right end of the gas tank—common practice with post-war hot rods. The added weight on the rear axle is a plus, of course, but more important it gets the battery out of that vulnerable, and unsightly, suspended hanger under the cockpit.

A neat battery box keeps everything tidy and isolates the battery from luggage and anything else you choose to carry in the trunk. We made our box from 18-gauge sheet metal, folded and welded—although riveted or bolted joints would work as well. We recommend a vent hole from the box to the underside of the body when using a conventional wet battery.

We would like to recommend something that's not in character with a traditional car but makes great sense for one that will probably be driven a lot less frequently than it would have when you were a youngster—assuming that you have reached codger status, as have most of us. Buy an Optima II battery for your hot rod. The Optima is a solid element battery (kind of like a gel cell only better) that is truly sealed, does not out-gas—at least not enough to cause problems—does not corrode, would start a Caterpillar D-8 in Nome in midwinter, and has a five-year guarantee. Yes, it's pricey, at nearly double the cost of a top-of-the-line DieHard or Interstate, but we feel that it's worth the extra 15 or so bucks a year. You'll never need a jump-start with this baby.

Trips down memory lane are a lot better without annoying reminders of the way some things really were.

The starter solenoid is located on a bracket under the right front corner of the body. It's out of sight but still reachable from the engine compartment.

The battery is carried in a steel case next to the gas tank. The positive cable connects to the solenoid and the negative cable is bolted to the transmission case to ensure a good ground.

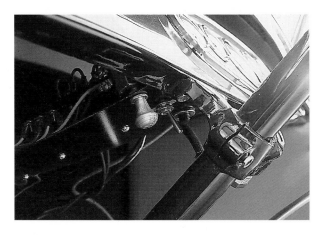

The headlight switch, starter button, and fuel pump shut-off switch are located on the underside of the electrical panel at the bottom of the dashboard.

Chapter 12

BELLS AND WHISTLES

CREATIVITY SHINES BRIGHT IN THE SPECIAL DETAILS

There was no resisting the showboat when it came down river with all its bells ringing and its whistles blowing. And there's no way to ignore a traditional hot rod with all the right "bells and whistles"—those wonderful details that make each rod special and unique.

The Bishop-Tardel Highboy has some bells and whistles of its own to make it different from other A-V8s, past, present, and even future. No matter how much we may like someone else's idea, it's impossible to resist adding our own wrinkles when we set out to duplicate that idea. If you choose to duplicate any of the B-T Highboy's bells or whistles, you'll doubtless add your own wrinkles

It's time to let the creative juices flow as you plan and make those special details that will personalize your hot rod.

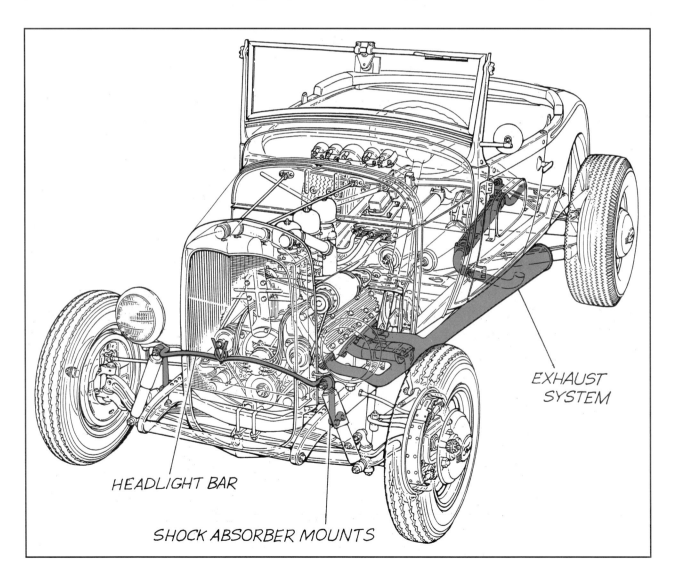

EXHAUST SYSTEM

HEADLIGHT BAR

SHOCK ABSORBER MOUNTS

and twists, thus making your car as distinct from ours as ours is from the hot rods that inspired it.

We've devoted a major part of an entire section to the exhaust system because it's probably the most prominent and important single feature on the B-T Highboy—the big bell, or whistle. To our eyes, the exhaust system makes the car!

We also include the construction details of some of the roadster's other nifty features, like the headlight bar, the front shock mounts, the raked windshield posts, and the hood. They're simply some more of the creative elements—the bells and whistles—that were part of the old-time roadsters.

EXHAUST SYSTEM

The exhaust system has its roots in some handsome A-V8s from the past—the Don Ferrara/Bill Rolland roadster that was a cover and feature car

1 In a progress mockup, the roadster looks okay, except for the large recess under the body side—just the place for a great-looking outside exhaust system...

2 A 1933–1934 torque tube and right-side header are used to mock up the system and locate the cone relative to the body and frame.

3 It's important to check mock-up details from all angles to ensure they look good. This is the important decision point for details this ambitious. The wide whites didn't make the "cut."

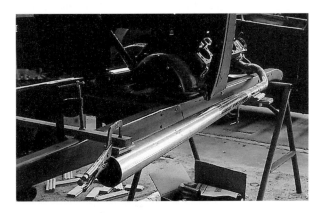

4 The cone is blocked and clamped in position prior to the start of fitting. We positioned the cones parallel to the frame rails, and 2 1/2 inches out and 1/2 inch down from the top.

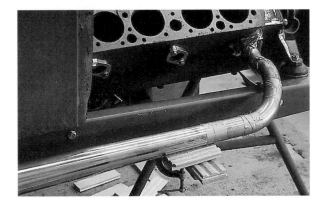

5 Wooden blocks support the forward end of the cone from beneath, so there won't be any interference with the fitting work.

numerous times, with at least two appearances in *Hot Rod* magazine, credited to its two best-known owners, and Dave Mitchell's award-winning roadster pickup that was one of the most-photographed hot rods of its time. These were two of the finest examples of postwar hot rod design and construction, their non-Deuce credentials notwithstanding. It's a reasonable assumption that the exhaust systems for these two as well as a handful of similarly adorned cars like Topper Chasse's impeccable Deuce-framed A-V8, were inspired by race car exhaust systems—track roadsters, Offy big cars, V-8-60 midgets. With smooth, gently curved head pipes flowing into long collectors, all bright and shiny, it's a great classic look.

The Method—Then and Now
While most race car external exhaust systems sported straight-tube collectors years ago, some clever hot-rodders took the big-tube look a step farther than the circle-track car guys, and used Ford torque-tube housings for exhaust system collectors—sort of super lakes pipes. Conservative rod builders at the time would cut a 1935–1936 driveshaft in two for a pair of neat, short cones. But for something really special, a pair of 1933–1934 driveline torque tubes was needed. With their near-constant taper these were the choice tubes; most of the torque tubes from other years start with a taper and transition into a long straight section, and although Model A torque tubes have a constant taper, they're also thick walled and rather heavy at better than 30 pounds apiece. Actually, all Ford torque tubes are relatively heavy and, when used as exhaust collectors, must be supported at the rear to prevent damage to the exhaust runners on the engine end of the system.

A torque-tube based system dictates mild steel runners and chrome plating. A buffed HPC finish would be a reasonable compromise, at about half the price of chrome today.

The biggest part of the plater's bill is for polishing in preparation for plating, so it pays to start with the very best torque tubes you can find. This isn't as easy as it was several decades ago, when perfect tubes could be purchased from wrecking yards for a couple of bucks. Old Ford torque tubes are no longer a wrecking yard staple, and those that have been lying around are usually badly pebbled with rust. During our hunt for 1933–1934 tubes, it became clear that the supply of good ones was thin at best; they've never been a high-demand part, and we suspect that most of them have been chucked out.

The system on the B-T Highboy is one solution to working around the scarce original tubes, although we admit that it's a pricey one, particu-

6 The rear of the cone is suspended from above. The wooden crosspiece was later replaced with steel angle iron to keep the cone from moving.

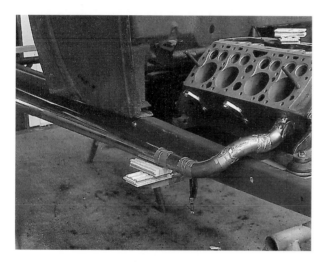

7 A plain steel mandrel-bent U-bend was used for trial fitting, and the segments were duct-taped together to give a us a feel for what the runner would look like. The stainless-steel exhaust flanges are bolted onto the block.

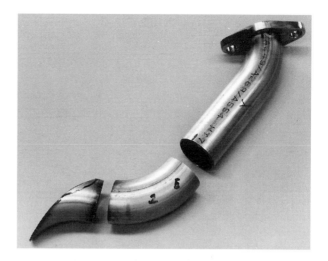

8 All the runners but one were made from three segments. With the exception of the end that's welded to the exhaust flange, all cuts are made perpendicular to the centerline of the tube to ensure precise fit of one segment to the next.

9 Each duckbill of the second and third runners was painstakingly fitted to the cone. The radius of the cone is different for each one.

larly in terms of early budget-built hot rods. But, not all the early rods were built on tight budgets, so our approach isn't without precedent.

The cost of material would have been much less if we had built the system in mild steel instead of stainless, but when we factored in the cost of plating a mild-steel system, the premium paid for the stainless was covered and then some. And as a big bonus, the stainless system can be easily repolished to remove heat discoloration and scratches and make it look brand new.

We've included a pattern and specifications for the cones. The 16-gauge, 304 stainless-steel cones were formed in halves on a press brake and then TIG welded together and metal finished on a

stake table. If all of that sounds like a foreign language, not to worry. This is highly specialized work, but it's still well within the capability of a competent custom sheet-metal shop.

The exhaust runners are made from six 1.75-inch-diameter 16-gauge 304 stainless-steel mandrel U-bends from Burns Stainless Steel (see Appendix A). The flanges were plasma cut from

3/8-inch stainless steel plate, using a flathead manifold gasket as a pattern.

The end caps are made from 3/4-inch 6061 aluminum plate, turned 1/4-inch larger in diameter than the end of the megaphone, and grooved to fit over the end and hold a seal. The caps, polished to get rid of any hint of an inappropriate billet-aluminum appearance, are held in place by a bolt that passes through a bar welded into the end of the megaphone.

The Work—Lots of It

There's no easy way to break this to you, but there is no easy way to build this exhaust system, no matter if you're using Ford torque tubes and muffler tubing or custom-made stainless-steel collectors and mandrel-bent runners.

But you will start a lot farther down the road toward completion than we did, because we're going to share all the stuff we had to dope out on our own. The folks who do this kind of work for a living—and do it well—get a ton of money for their efforts and earn every penny of it. We were given some valuable ground rules and hints by Rod Sexton, who is arguably one of the finest custom exhaust system builders on the planet, and we've folded Rod's help into our story.

Mock It Up

It all begins in mockup, with the major pieces of the car tied together, sitting on the correct wheels

10 The first runner on the right side has been fitted and tacked in place. Things were beginning to get easier at this stage.

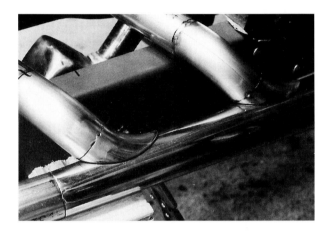

12 Note how the duckbill fits down over the cone. Later, the opening in the cone will be cut, leaving a 1/8-inch ledge to prevent blowthrough during welding.

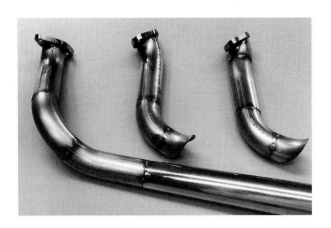

11 The left side runners, all fitted and tacked together. The third runner required a fourth section at the exhaust flange to clear the steering box.

13 A simple aluminum clamp with holes punched in it helps hold the segments together for tacking.

and tires, just as you want it to sit on the road. We mocked up the B-T Highboy with a 1934 torque tube and a right-side tube header on the left side of the car. This allowed us to position the big cone right where we wanted it, and use the sweep of the right-side header runners to suggest the appearance of the final system. We liked what we saw—after better than an hour of argument and debate and moving the system elements around with shims and blocks and clamps and bits of wire. But that's OK, just as it was when we were kids and all our buddies attempted to over-lay their ideas onto our visions. Now it's our turn to do it just the way we want!

Choose a Comfortable Method

There are several ways to build this type of ex-haust system. If you're a tube-bending kind of guy with your own mandrel bender, or access to one, you'll probably make the runners in contin-uous lengths. And if you're an old-school fabrica-tor you may be thinking about sand-bending the runners. If one or both of these methods are vi-able options for you, there's probably very little that we can tell you from here on. But if you're like most of us, welded-segment fabrication is the easiest approach; you don't have to dope out an entire runner all at one time, and it doesn't re-quire years of experience to produce clean-flow-ing runners.

Setup

Before we began fitting the system, we installed the engine block in the frame on fresh motor-mount pads; there's not a lot of distance be-tween the exhaust runners and the frame, so it's essential that the engine is in its final position before any fitting work is started. Also, we in-stalled the steering box, with the pitman arm and sector shaft nut, so we could establish the correct clearance between the system and the steering on the left side.

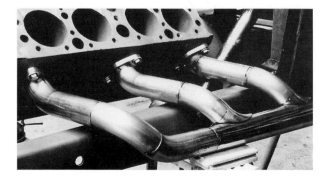

14 A final check fit of assembled runners and the cone is made prior to finish welding.

We had the first couple of feet of the for-ward ends of the cones polished at a plating shop before starting work because it makes final pol-ishing easier later on. Then, we positioned the left cone parallel to the frame rail with the for-ward end 1/2 inch out from the sector shaft nut and the rear end of the cone about 4 inches from the frame rail. The forward end was supported with a 1/2-inch block on a crosspiece clamped to the bottom of the frame rails. The rear of the cone was spaced 1/2 inch down from the top of the frame rail with a crosspiece laid across and clamped to the top of the frame. Then, with the left cone in place, we positioned the right cone, duplicating the distances and clearances from the left side.

We next bolted the runner flanges to the block with fresh gaskets and cinched them down. And now, things got scary; it was time to make that first cut and begin fitting the first ex-haust runner!

Fitting

We used $12 muffler-tube mandrel U-bends for trial fitting rather than learn on $25 stainless-steel bends, and we'd recommend the same for anyone short of Rod Sexton's ability. While we're not talking about a lot of money in the overall scheme, there's something special and even in-timidating about stainless steel. We were a lot more relaxed hacking away at the plain stuff.

Exhaust Tip One—

Before we get into the actual fitting we want to share what we feel is the single most important hint from Rod, and that is to make all tubing cuts square, as in perpendicular to the centerline of the tube. This ensures that you are fitting a circle to a circle rather than trying to match a circle to an ellipse, or trying to mate dissimilar ellipses.

Having said that, we're going to tell you that we cheated on our first cut, where the runner starts at the flange on the block, and cut them with about a 5-degree bias. Here it's OK because the tub-ing diameter is a little larger than the hole in the flange, and a little cheating is necessary to turn the runner up to horizontal as soon as possible; the down-angled exhaust outlets in the flathead block are only a few inches above the frame rails.

We made all of our cuts on a bandsaw with a Diemaster 1/2-inch-wide, .025-gauge, 14-TPI (teeth-per-inch) steel-cutting blade. We were given the specs by pro metalman Walt Letherman, the fellow who fabricated our cones, and it was great advice. Months later, after making countless cuts in hard stainless steel tubing, the same blade con-tinued to work like new, cutting mild steel tubing as if it were plastic and aluminum, almost as quickly as we could move the material.

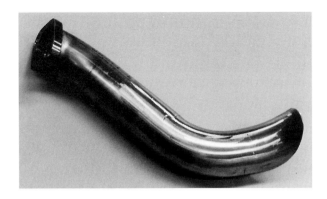

15 After the segments of each runner are welded together, the weld is ground down and low spots are built up with additional weld before being sent to the polisher.

16 The polished cones and runners are assembled on the chassis prior to final welding. The polisher loved doing the work in stages, and it saved some money as well.

17 The joints are undetectable, giving each runner the look of being made from a continuous tube.

18 The weld at the runner-to-cone joints is built up so it can be blended during final polishing.

19 After welding is completed, the cone is blocked into its final position for normalizing. This cone had risen 1/2 inch and moved inward 2 inches during welding!

20 Heat was applied to the cone opposite of the runner weld joints. The heat patterns are visible on the bottom of the cone. When the cone cooled, the wood blocks fell to the floor. Amazing!

OK, so we've been avoiding the work, and you're about to discover why. As we said, there's no easy way to build this exhaust system. You must visualize the path from the block to the cone, picturing how you want it to flow, and then picturing each of the elements that makes up that path. The runner shown, all in pieces, is the result of hours of cut-and-try fitting. Subsequent runners took a lot less time and the job actually turned into fun toward the end.

We added a level of complexity that isn't entirely necessary, with the duck-bill blends into the cone on the second and third runners. We did it this way because it's an elegant solution—optimum with regard to performance—and it was the blended headers of high-end race motors that influenced postwar hot-rodders. The runner junctions can also be made with a straight section of runner intersecting the cone, but it's not as pretty and not as efficient. On our headers, after several thousand miles there's no indication of "hot-spots" at any of the junctions. There is only the faintest, uniform gold cast that starts at the flanges and quickly fades in just a few inches along each of the runners.

Once the runner feet are fitted and trimmed to sit on the surface of the cone, their outlines are marked and an opening is cut into the cone, leaving a ledge of 3/32 to 1/8 inch to provide some metal to weld to without blow-throughs.

We TIG welded our stainless system with stainless rod, and built up the junctions with fillet so the runners could be blended with the cone during polishing.

Exhaust Tip Two—
Here's a tip we figured out by ourselves, one that the polisher loved, and that was to let them polish the completed individual runners before they were welded to the big tubes. It made the polishing work a whole lot easier and resulted in a very high level of quality at a superreasonable price.

Normalizing the System
All final welding was done with the runners bolted to the block to maintain all the elements in alignment, as much as possible. Then, after all the fitting and welding was done, and before final polishing, the exhaust system had to be normalized—or stress relieved or whatever you choose to call it—so the big cones returned to where we first positioned them. Make no mistake, we're talking about some major repositioning; the rear ends of the cones didn't move just a few thou' or even 1/4 or 1/2 inch in one direction. These beauties moved around big time. One had risen 1/2 inch and moved inward toward the frame 2 inches! The other side was a little better, but still a long way from where it had started. Veteran tinman Terry Schank was the man who TIG'd the system for us, and he was the obvious person to set matters straight, seeing as how he's logged a bazillion hours building headers and exhaust systems. With Terry's guidance, we blocked the cones back to their original locations using wedges and levers and all manner of force. Not to worry; if the welds are good, the stainless will handle deflection. Terry then applied heat to select points on the cones, and while he was telling us that as soon as the headers had taken their correct set, the blocks that held them in place would drop out, the blocks did just that and fell to the floor! Smoke and mirrors? No, just a lot of experience, the kind of experience you should look for when you're building your exhaust system. It may look easy, but trust us when we tell

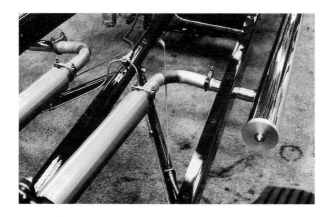

The bypass tubes from the cones angle up and connect to the mufflers through 90-degree elbows. Later, with the body in place, hangers connected to the bypass tubes will support the rear of the headers.

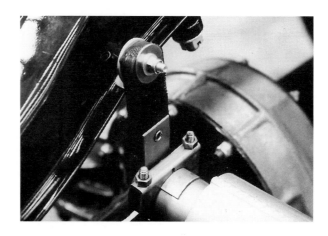

Smithy's mufflers are suspended from the rear cross-member with conventional muffler hangers attached with L-brackets. Later, hangers will suspend the front of the mufflers from a hat channel under the floor of the body.

you it isn't. Still, the results are worth the cost and the effort, and you don't have to trust us for that; you can see for yourself.

Alternate Approaches
The headers and pipes for a high-end A-V8 can also be made from individual runners into a 3-into-1 collector that connects to a commercially available, large-diameter straight-tube section. This, in fact, was the type of system on the Ferrara/Rolland roadster, using a method common at the time for fabricating flathead V-8 track roadster/sprint car headers. As with the B-T Highboy

The attachment for the cone end cap is made of stainless tube and barstock welded in position. A bolt is used rather than a stud so it can be easily replaced if it's damaged.

The end caps are 3/4-inch 6061 aluminum plate that's 1/4 inch larger than the diameter of the cone. A groove cut in the face of the plate holds a heavy bead of high-temp RTV that forms a seal.

system, this one can be made up in mild steel or stainless (both mild steel and stainless collectors are available from Burns Stainless). The welded-segment method is probably the best in this type of system as it was with ours, although old photos

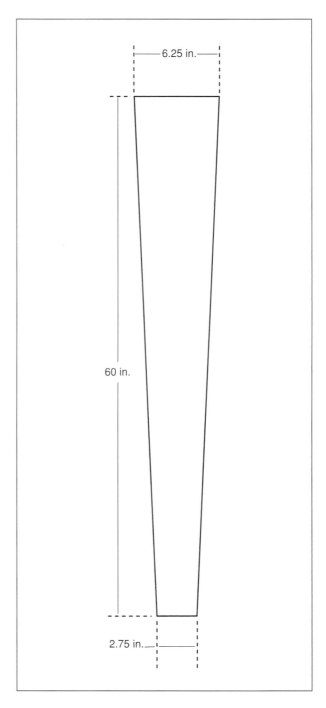

The cone halves are formed in a press brake, with the brake head offset (angled), and each progressive strike made in a radial pattern.

we've seen of Dave Mitchell doing this sort of work show smooth, one-piece runners that were either mandrel or sand-bent; the good part is that you're dealing with definite A-to-B points, which makes it relatively easy to bridge the long gap between the motor and the big megaphone.

Mufflers and Pipes

Selecting mufflers for a traditional 1950 hot rod is easy enough; they have to be Smithy's—what else? Thanks to Tony DiCosta at Hot Rod Supply in Florida, brand-new Smithy's glasspacks, just like the originals, are not only available but for less money than you'd pay for most modern turbo-style mufflers.

We rotated the bypass tubes from the collectors up about 7–10 degrees to tuck the mufflers up between the frame rails. A 90-degree elbow connects each bypass to its respective muffler, which is supported from the rear cross-member with a garden-variety muffler hanger. A second hanger at the forward end of each muffler supports the muffler as well as the rear of the big cone. The tailpipes are straight sections that were "dog-legged" on a muffler-shop bender, using a length of welding rod bent into a pattern for the muffler-shop fellow to follow. Finally, a pair of 1 3/4-inch "pencil" tips were MIG welded to the ends of the tailpipes.

SHOCK ABSORBER MOUNTS

While many hot rods were still depending on OEM Houdaille 50/50 lever-arm shocks for wheel control into the early 1950s, the hot setup was "airplane shocks." In reality these were the common telescopic hydraulically damped units the industry has used for decades. But back then they were sort of trick, and they worked a lot better than old, tired 50/50s.

Telescopic shocks were also cheaper to manufacture, and by 1947 cost-conscious Ford had made the switch on both passenger cars and light trucks. Ford also began producing a handsome shock absorber mount that was almost made to order for hot rods. With just a bit of heat and coaxing, this elegant forging provided a strong upper shock mount on the frame—and looked great at the same time. It's interesting that the shock mount came from the F-1 pickup truck; the passenger car piece is a clunky, homely stamping that has no business out in the sunlight!

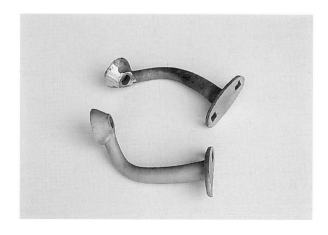

1 One half of a Model A headlight bar is clamped to the frame horn in preparation for bending. The center of the bar provides a great handle for doing the job.

2 The mount is heated and slowly bent into shape until the headlight socket is horizontal. The opposite mount is bent the same way, using the height of the first one as a guide to make them even.

3 With the center bar cut off and the sockets blended, these new mounts are ready for polishing and plating.

The base holes on the F-1 mount are too far apart for slim Model A and Deuce rails, but this is easily resolved in a couple of ways. First, you can either heat the mount above the top mounting hole and bend the upper portion of the mount back in a smooth arc until the mounting holes are horizontal. Or, you can cut the lower part of the mount off just below the top mounting hole, rotate the bottom piece up until it's perpendicular to the upper part, and weld it back together.

We used the second method for the B-T Highboy because we also wanted the shock mounts to serve double duty and provide a base for headlight mounts. Also, the taller, straight mount resulting from this approach is more complementary to the A-V8's strong vertical lines. The shock mounts are installed with Grade 8 7/16-inch bolts, using the original rivet holes—enlarged—where the front cross-member connects to the frame rails. This provides a double thickness of frame material to support the load on the shock absorbers.

The lower shock mount, at the axle, is a bung welded to the front of the axle perch pin boss and threaded to accept a screw-in shock mounting stud. It couldn't be simpler.

HEADLIGHT MOUNTS

Headlights are a major visual element on just about any car, and on a highboy roadster, where there are no dominant fenders, the headlights become an even stronger style element.

It's not so much a trick in placing the headlights in the right location as it is skill in avoiding the pitfalls of poor placement. Place them too high and you have the frog look—kind of silly and probably not what you had in mind through all those months and years planning your dream rod. Set them too low and the car has a head-down look—as well as a second look from John Law, who will pull you over to the side of the road to make sure the lights are above the legal minimum height—which they probably are not.

Place the lights too close to the radiator shell and the car looks cross-eyed, too far away and it has a walleyed look. And don't discount the size of the lights themselves. Itty-bitty lights give a highboy a beady-eyed character, and big flat-lens lamps produce a myopic stare.

1 The B-T Highboy shock absorber mounts are described in Chapter Three. They also serve as the headlight mounts.

2 The ends of the headlight bar are the "feet" of a 1932 bar with one ear removed and the arc heated and bent to match the cross-section of the radiator shell. The 1932 headlight sockets are trimmed and welded to the top of the shock mounts.

One of the early guarantees for success in headlight location and mounting was the handsome strut-type cast-aluminum mount produced by several companies in the 1950s, including speed-equipment giants like Offenhauser. These mounts look as great today as they did back then, and reasonably good copies are currently available from companies like Hot Rod and Custom Supply and Speedway Motors.

Or, you can do as most early rodders did, and as we did for the B-T Highboy, and make your own headlight mounts from existing Ford hardware.

While we eventually added our headlight mounts to the front shock mounts, we first took a look at one of the most common and effective of the old-time solutions and made a set of mounts from a Model A headlight bar. For this exercise, simply cut the headlight bar in two in the middle, then clamp the ends to the frame rails where you will eventually install them. Next, heat the bar evenly between the headlight socket and the mount, and bend the bar into position using the long stub as a handle. When you think the socket is positioned just about right, install a headlight

bucket and check its position. Then, when you're happy with the first one, do the other side the same way. After the mounts have cooled, cut off the excess center bar and shape the outside of the socket with a grinder. That's it; you have a pair of headlight mounts ready to bolt to the frame rails after they're painted or plated.

HEADLIGHT BARS

Headlight bars were popular for the early highboys not only for their style but because they were practical; by tying the headlights together, a headlight bar all but eliminates the annoying flutter of a couple of unrelated lights bobbing around on long stalks. Interestingly, headlight bars weren't used with the cast-aluminum headlight mounts, which have also been known to flutter.

Headlight bars are probably not as unique as fingerprints, although there is certainly some kinship with cattle brands, in which the owner strives for identity within the constraints of what's required of the device and how much space it will occupy.

Creating a headlight bar is one of those great Saturday projects that you do with a pal or

3 The center of the headlight bar is the center of the original 1932 bar. It retains the original arc and is bent back to follow the cross-section of the Deuce grille. Even the 1932 V-8 emblem was used.

The windshield posts were piecut about 3/16 inch, beginning at the rear, leaving the front face intact. They were then bent back and installed on the car for a preliminary check for appearance and fit.

two on hand, after the mockup of the car has all the major elements in place. You can make a bar the way we did for the B-T highboy, using an existing stock headlight bar—in this case a 1932 Commercial—or construct it from quarter-inch plate and heavy-wall tubing. The only rules are make it yours and make it fun.

WINDSHIELD POSTS

The B-T Highboy debuted at the Oakland Roadster Show and attended several major events with one of its significant details still in question. When the car was in the mockup stage Vern and Bill Grainger suggested raking the windshield, but I resisted because I had always liked the Ferrara/Holland car with its unraked chopped windshield. My resolve began to flag when I discovered that the car looked great at some angles and not so great at others. When all key elements are right, a car will look good from all angles.

I began to question my decision about the windshield when we had the car in the studio for the *American Rodder* magazine feature photography; it looked just a bit too prim and proper. The whole matter came to a head at the First Muroc Reunion, when the roadster was parked next to an old prewar highboy with a severely raked windshield; even the uniform dusting of dry-lake talc couldn't overcome the blue car's dude look.

Raking the windshield is truly a cut-and-try process, whether you're working with original posts or stainless steel replacement posts like ours. With the posts removed from the car, we bandsawed a 1/8-inch pie-cut from the rear, about 1/4 inch above the top screw hole, leaving the front face of the post intact. We were looking for about 10–12 degrees of rake, and when we bent the top of the post back it was at about 8 degrees. Removing another thin 1/16-inch sliver did the trick, and we tacked the post and cut the opposite one the same amount, tacked it then installed the windshield to check for appearance and fit.

Both were on the money.

Stainless ace Gary Henshaw TIG welded the posts and then carefully ground and polished them back to their original finish. The stainless posts are the easiest and least expensive to work with, in that they don't need to be replated.

So, a couple hours of work and the B-T Highboy looks great from all angles—more aggressive, racy, and right. Putting it in contemporary vernacular, Vern says the roadster now has "attitude."

Once everything was okay, the posts were TIG welded back together, then ground smooth and polished.

The raked windshield gives the B-T Highboy some essential "attitude."

Chapter 13

INTERIOR AND TOP

HANDSOME AND PRACTICAL

Almost done, the roadster needs only a comfortable—and attractive—interior to be a complete, first-rate traditional hot rod. With the addition of a good top to the package, the fun time increases.

Hot rod interiors in the postwar era were simple, functional, and suited to the rigors of rodding. Woven fabrics were for your grandparents, and a new pleat 'n roll job in leather or that wonderful new Naugahyde stuff was high on most rodders' priority lists. With a couple of decades of exposure and wear, original "leatherette" interiors were in pretty poor condition, and replacement upholstery from LeBaron Bonney didn't even exist. The restoration hobby was just starting to get interested in Model As and Deuces, and the repro parts industry was still somewhere off in the future.

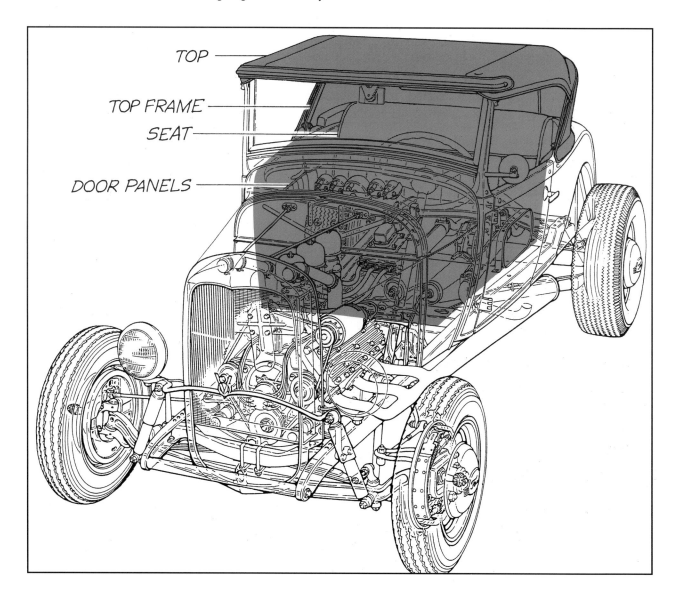

TOP

TOP FRAME

SEAT

DOOR PANELS

The definitive pleat-and-roll California hot rod interior was a takeoff on upholstery schemes lavished on expensive cars. The pleats alone consumed as much as one-third more material than flat-panel upholstery, so it was not a treatment seen in low-priced new cars. But the rich look was too hard to resist when having a custom interior stitched up. The added cost for pleats in a small cockpit amounted to little more than a couple of overtime Sundays pumping gas at the service station.

SOME BASIC GUIDELINES

Rolled and pleated upholstery—also called tuck and roll—was equally popular in customs and saw some of its greatest expression in the tail draggers. Some of the schemes, like "horseshoe" rolls, don't always translate from the spacious interior of a custom coupe to the small cockpit of a roadster, however, where straight rolls provide the same richness and can actually make the cockpit appear larger. Nonetheless, there have been some handsome roadster interiors stitched together over the years featuring horseshoe rolls. It's mostly a matter of scale, with rolls of 5 to 7 inches wide and 2- to 2 1/2-inch pleats working best.

Straight pleat or stitched upholstery—like original Model A and '32 interiors—was much in evidence in the postwar cars with some of it carried over from prewar reupholstery jobs. It's still a great look.

Roadster interior colors tended to favor tans and browns, black, oxblood, and an occasional bright red, often with contrasting white or black. All colors were fair game, of course, and brighter colors and two-tone interiors began to turn up with increasing regularity as the 1950s got underway.

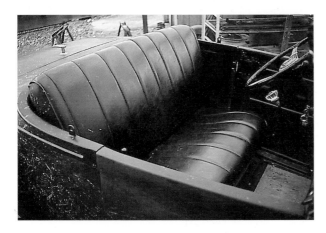

Original Model A roadster seat from a 30-year-old restoration works well in this cockpit, because the large body cross-rib has been removed and the seat frame is on the floor. The imitation leather upholstery and straight stitched "pleats" give Bill Grainger's highboy a true postwar character.

SEATS AND PANELS

Reproduction Model A seat springs are available through most of the old-Ford parts sources. They fit the stock body, of course, but gobble up all sorts of interior room. Remember, these cars were designed for generally poor roads, and much of the "suspension" was designed into the seat cushions.

There's no longer a need for this sort of cushion—nor did postwar hot-rodders feel that there was at that time; built-up seats on plywood bases were common and actually preferred because of the lower seating position.

We took a look at both options for the B-T Highboy and chose the built-up seat approach. The Model A cushions were much too full, and there's no practical way to cut or tie them down. Old pros, including one who worked for Bill Harrah for years, warned against modifications to the spring cushions; they simply will not last.

Our seat and backrest bases are made of 5/8-inch exterior grade plywood, cut 1/4-inch smaller all around than the seat frame and the width of the rear of the cockpit. We drilled a dozen 1/2-inch holes in each panel to allow the cushions to breathe, and then painted the bases body color before turning the job over to the upholsterer.

We later upgraded the bottom cushion by cutting out the center under each of the two seating positions, turning the base into a frame with 3 inches of wood all around and in the center. We then bridged the openings with a lattice of Pirelli furniture webbing, pulled tight and stapled on the underside of the seat base before reattaching the leather. The seat comfort, which had been good, was now excellent—as good as a metal-spring seat.

The door, seat side, and kick panels are made of 1/8-inch plywood "doorskin" that can be found at any full-service lumber yard. The finished panels—based on paper patterns we made from butcher's paper—were given a couple of clear coats to seal them against moisture. Unlike conventional automotive "cardboard" backing, which begins to warp almost as soon as it's put in place, the sealed wood will retain its shape for years and no doubt outlast the upholstery material.

MATERIAL CHOICES

Your choice of material is a personal decision. Whether it's leather or vinyl matters not so much as the finish. For leather, either smooth or textured is OK, because that's about the only way leather is tanned. Synthetics available in the postwar world were primarily textured leatherettes and Naugahyde, in either lightly textured or smooth finish.

At the time, Naugahyde was as desirable as leather because it was new and " . . . virtually in-

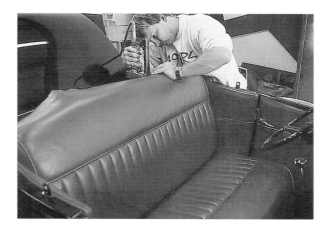

1 The seat bottom in the B-T Highboy is about 2 inches lower than a stock Model A seat. An extra 1 inch of horizontal space could be harvested by removing the wood seat-back support behind the finisher at the top of the cockpit.

4 We opted to have the seat-back upholstery rolled over onto the wood rail at the rear of the cockpit. The seat back can still be removed by unscrewing the nuts that hold the wood rail to the body.

2 Upholsterer Jack Buchanan checks the built-up seat back for room and comfort. Make yourself available during this phase of interior work so the cockpit can be fitted to you.

3 Jack added a vinyl finisher panel to the back of the seat back because it can be seen when the deck lid is open—not absolutely essential but a very neat touch when it's all done.

5 Red "Hydem" strip covers the trimmed and stapled edge of the seat-back upholstery to complete the job.

destructible." (And our cities would soon be lighted with free atomic power!) Truth to tell, Naugahyde was great stuff. It didn't stain like leather, it was cheaper, and there were many great colors available.

Leather is readily available from suppliers such as Bill Hirsch (see Appendix A), and Naugahyde and Naugahyde-like vinyls are everywhere. Leatherette-style fabrics are also available from restoration supply specialists, but they're often as costly as top-quality leather—and not as durable.

1 The stock 1930–1931 Deluxe top frame was too high and too long for the body after the windshield was chopped and raked back. The height was corrected by cutting 2 1/2 inches off the bottom of the main-bow irons, drilling a new mounting hole, and recontouring the end.

3 The chopped and shortened top frame fits fine after a couple hours of surgery. The posts that the frame connects to at the top of the windshield must be bent forward to compensate for the rake of windshield.

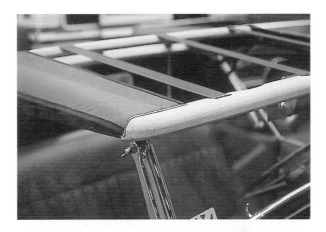

2 To correct the length, we cut the horizontal frame apart, mounted the front half on the windshield, overlapped the cut ends to determine the amount to be trimmed, then welded the frame back together after the excess was cut off.

4 Like any good-quality convertible top, this one begins with webs and padding tacked to the wood header and bows.

TOP—EXTENDING THE FUN

Wander back in time with Don Montgomery's books or old issues of *Hot Rod* magazine to look at the roadsters in postwar California and there are only a couple of conclusions to be drawn about weather protection: Either very few roadsters had tops, or maybe they all did but no one took pictures in bad weather.

Tops were far more common than the photo record indicates, even in sunny southern California where winter rains often last for days at a time throughout several months. With a roadster as their sole transportation, many hot-rodders would have found the going a bit tough, were it not for a top and even a set of side curtains for many.

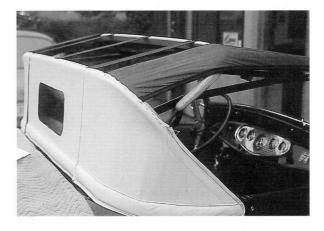

5 The snaps around the rear of the top and window are hidden under a padded 2-inch roll, just as they were on many Bob Lee tops in the 1950s.

A top isn't just for wet or cold weather. In fact, a light-color top provides welcome shade in hot weather, and with the rear window unzipped it's almost as breezy as no top.

Most often, the top was left up while it was on the car, and many didn't fold at all, even when based on a stock frame and bows that had been cut down to fit a chopped windshield.

For the B-T Highboy, we started with a stock 1930–1931 Deluxe roadster top, because the frame is solid barstock that can either be redrilled or cut and welded to alter the shape of the top. The 1928–1929 top, as well as the one for the 1930–1931 Standard roadster, has conical sheet-metal bows that are difficult to chop. The later top frame is also cleaner appearing, with only its main rear bow exposed below the curtain flap on the side.

Taking our cues from photos of tops made by Pasadena trimmer Bob Lee in the 1940s and 1950s, we recontoured the frame to fit the chopped and raked windshield, and dropped the crown slightly for a more-aggressive profile. The top was covered in white pinpoint top fabric that's much like the synthetics that were introduced in the late 1940s. We had considered American Stayfast top fabric, which has the body and richness of canvas without its shortcomings, but it's not available in white—absolutely essential for our proper Bob Lee–style lid.

Side curtains should be made of the same material as the top, with flexible Lexan "windows," and mounted on custom frames made from 1/4-inch cold-rolled steel rod.

There's no rule that says a top is a must-have on a traditional hot rod, but it certainly increases its utility—and extends the driving season for the car.

Rain and sun protection and a great traditional look all come together in a top styled to fit the car.

Chapter 14

EPILOGUE

ONE YEAR LATER

When Vern Tardel and I started the Bishop-Tardel Highboy roadster and book project, it didn't occur to us that the car would be finished more than a year before the book went to the printer, but that's because I have a good deal more ongoing optimism than day-to-day stick-to-itiveness. I envisioned a gap of no more than three months, four months tops, before we would be shipping books all over the world. Placing total trust in me for the book side of the project, Vern went along with my timetable, although I'm certain that after 22 months of working together on the roadster, during which time he had come to recognize my proclivity toward periods of sloth and inertia, his agreement was more from politeness than any real belief that I would make the book happen when I said. Building the roadster, Vern knew where to push and how to move things along; for the book he had only my word to go on.

Finished!
Twenty-two months after the first parts were sandblasted, the B-T Highboy is ready to turn a wheel outside for the first time.

Vern turns Bluey around for its first trip down the avenue. My preoccupation with the ground is a cover-up for what was a rather emotional moment. Remember, this is a 42-year-old dream that's about to become real!

But something good has come of the delay, although I won't kid you that I planned it this way. That is that we've had a year to live with the roadster, a year to nurse it through the inevitable teething problems and refine it into a better hot rod than we could have told you about if I'd gotten my butt in gear early on. I've even named the roadster, something I'm not inclined to do with my cars, even those I love. I call it Bluey, mostly because of its color, but also because of some special memories I share with my daughters involving a family cat with the same name. Don't ask; you had to be there.

Anyway, some of the improvements were cranked right into the draft without fanfare because they were minor little tweaks that weren't worth belaboring. Others are talked about, however, because they deal with the sort of choices hot-rodders make when planning and building cars.

Just as important, we have a year's worth of driving experiences to share with you and let you know that you're in for a great deal of fun, should you choose to build a traditional high-boy roadster. Lest you think that a correct post-war hot rod means living with compromised comfort, performance, and utility, I'm here to tell you 'tain't so, McGee; this roadster is one of the unfussiest fun/performance cars I've driven, including a few from the muscle-car era and some "upgraded" modern street rods. The formula for success seems to have something to do with balance. At just a shade more than 2,000 pounds, and with about 175 flatmotor horsepower and 200 foot-pounds of torque to move it

The day before Oakland and John Castetter "clocks" fasteners while Bill Grainger touches up assembly chips.

Set up day at the Oakland Roadster Show, nice and dry now and ready for a last-minute shine.

144

along, Bluey is satisfyingly quick and fast. In terms of quarter-mile performance, I'd guess an ET in the mid-15s with trap speed in the 90s. Steering effort is appropriately low, and braking force—with four large Lincoln/Bendix stoppers on duty—is astounding. I doubt that discs would do any better.

The ride, which started out way stiff in the rear, improved very little with use, so we lightened up the rear spring by removing another leaf and installing softer shocks. This helped, but the big gain came from adding about 200 pounds of ballast to the rear of the frame and body. The sprung weight of the rear of a highboy A-V8 roadster is probably no more (or maybe even less) than the unsprung weight. As a result, there's

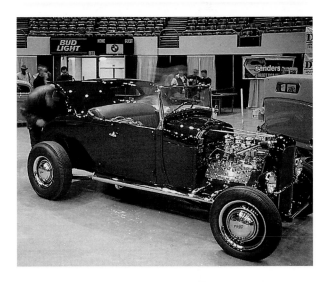

All done and ready for space assignment.

Bluey wound up in a dark hallway between the main arena and the display hall. "Lots of snack bar traffic," everyone said reassuringly.

simply not enough normal mass to "work" the rear suspension. The addition of sprung weight does wonders for ride performance.

The front also benefited with a switch to softer shock absorbers, and handling performance is much better than one would expect from a buggy-spring car. Body roll is almost imperceptible on corners, and the little fellow can be confidently hustled through the twisties right up to the breakaway point of its old-style rubber, which is signaled well in advance of things going wrong. We've yet to investigate Bluey's performance with radial tires, and frankly have some reservations about them; the high breakaway point of radials seems to need supple suspension to avoid surprises. We did switch from 5.00x16 motorcycle tires on the front to 4.50/4.75x16 Firestone passenger car tires from Coker. The motorcycle tires, with their rounded crown, developed an odd wear pattern that began to show up at around 5,000 miles and then rapidly worsened in the next couple of thou'. Even more important, motorcycle tires aren't designed to operate at a slip angle, which probably explains the beginning of tread separation between the ribs, around the circumference of the tire. So, save yourself some grief—and some dollars—and pass on motorcycle tires in favor of passenger car rubber.

The new 'Stones are Deluxe Champions, like the big wienies on the rear, so there's a more unified look about the car than there was before. Particularly nice is the quality of this recreation of what is arguably one of the handsomest tires ever made. Best of all, the new passenger car tires ride and handle way better with greatly reduced steering effort.

THE ROLLOUT

We finished Bluey four days before the Oakland Roadster Show in January 1996. The promoters had reserved a spot for us after accepting the car based on photos taken in October, during the late stages of construction. Had the car been completed much earlier or later in the year than the Oakland show it's doubtful that we would have entered it; it was built to drive and we weren't about to wait around for more than a couple of weeks to wring it out.

As things turned out, we had an opportunity to wring it out, literally, before Oakland. On the night before the show, we rolled Bluey into a borrowed race car trailer after a day spent polishing and detailing the little rascal, just minutes before we were smacked with a classic northern California river-raiser of a storm. It wasn't until the next morning that we discovered that the trailer leaked—a lot! The first hour of set-up day at the roadster show was spent drying everything so we could polish it again. No big deal.

Looking back, that first rain episode may have been an omen of what was ahead. During

Viewed from the landing above it at Oakland, the little blue car looked like a scale model.

Home in its own garage for the first time. It's time to bring home the tools from Vern's.

two trips in the fall of 1997, plus another one over the Thanksgiving holiday in 1998, Bluey logged 16 hours on the road in pouring rain—more water than most street rods see in their life-time, including wash jobs! But, again, it's no big deal because it hasn't dissolved the critter and he dries off and cleans up just fine.

Not surprisingly, the roadster was a bit of a puzzle for some showgoers at Oakland in 1996—and at least one judge who saw it as a clean, but near-stock Model A with a later engine! But this picture is already changing as more traditional style cars are built and shown. Promoters are already adding classes for traditional hot rods now that the trend is clear. Anyway, Bluey did us proud, receiving a class award and a crotch-high trophy to prove we were there.

AN ERRAND-RUNNIN' GROCERY GETTER
Long before the 1996 rodding season got under-way, Bluey was on the street, running film to the photo lab for processing, commuting from my house to Vern's shop for work sessions on other projects, hitting an occasional cruise night, and, yes, actually used for trips to the grocery store on a regular basis.

The busy staging lanes at Sears Point Raceway, the Jim Davis Memorial Goodguys/VRA drags. We've just unhooked Charley Brown's flathead dragster from Bluey and wait for the call to the line.

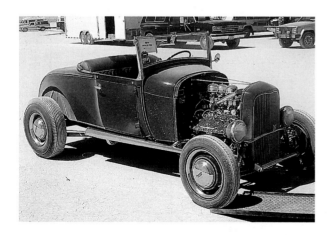

Edwards Air Force Base for the First Muroc Reunion. What's a nice car like Bluey doing in a place like this? Having fun!

When the Goodguys/VRA Nostalgia Drag Racing season got under way, Bluey shared race track tow-car duty with Vern's Deuce highboy for a mutual pal's flathead dragster. The roadster was on hand at several of the Goodguys fairground events in California and even picked up an award at Merced. Its picture appeared in several magazines, and of course there was a major story in *American Rodder*, for which I wrote regularly as a feature editor.

When I took Bluey to Edwards Air Force Base for the First Muroc Reunion, there were some who thought I'd taken leave of my senses. The dry-lake silt coats cars inside and out and resists attempts to dislodge it with air pressure alone. But the few hours spent in cleanup when I returned home was a small price to pay for the attaboys and smiles the little blue car garnered in the company of bona fide hot rods and hot-rodders from the past.

The next big event for the season was the L.A. Roadsters' Show on Father's Day at Pomona, and once again Bluey was warmly received and thoroughly enjoyed. On Friday evening of that weekend I bopped by Bob's Big Boy drive-in in Toluca Lake, a favorite watering hole when I was a callow youth, and was transported back to a teenage fantasy: "It's Friday night, I'm at Bob's, and I've got this cool roadster."

Back home in northern California, I drove Bluey to Andy's Last Picnic, only an hour away, where I introduced the roadster to Tom Medley, whose "Stroker McGurk" cartoons provided so much inspiration for this car when I first began to think about it as a kid. Tom loved the car and was all over and under it, checking out details and taking pictures for his own scrapbook.

The official season in the West ended with the California Hot Rod Reunion staged by the NHRA at Famoso dragstrip north of Bakersfield,

and Bluey was on hand, part of a four-roadster caravan that wandered down from Northern California.

As it has been since it started four years earlier, this reunion was bigger and better, with a lot of the "better" for me this time coming from being there in my own reunion-appropriate roadster. I'm proud to say that Bluey is a no-apologies hot rod that's perfectly at-home among the oldsters in spite of his youth. Some of the old guys were fooled by it, and even those who weren't were nevertheless appreciative that we went to such lengths to recreate a pure postwar SoCal highboy in every detail.

The high-point of the reunion weekend came when one of the old-timers admiring Bluey turned out to be Don Ferrara. His recognition of the similarity of Bluey to his roadster was praise and tribute beyond any I had imagined. In a wonderful long conversation we had, Don recounted details of some of the work on his roadster—as clearly remembered and related as if it

Gary Henshaw and I wait for clearance from the tow-car lane steward to retrieve Charley Brown's digger at Sears Point again during the Fall Classic drags.

had been done just the week before—and I reflected on how similar our work had been building Bluey, right down to the specs and details. The experience was so special that even the trip home in 6 1/2 hours of steady rain was pure adventure—no annoyance.

Bluey's last adventure for the first year was a SoCal based research trip for feature stories for *American Rodder* magazine, beginning with an in-

Bakersfield for the NHRA Reunion, in good highboy company. From left, the Deuce of Bob Stewart (L'il Axle); Vern's Deuce; Jack Lowe's 1928 Ford, "Monkey-Motion"; Bluey; and Mike Russell's Moomjean Auto Sales Deuce—all flatties 'cept Lowe's Chebby motor.

terview with hot rod artist/racer Bob McCoy at his studio home east of San Diego. Veteran rodder Bob Stewart whose dad, Ed Stewart (Axle), gave hot-rodding the Dago axle, was next on our agenda, just a couple of hours north of San Diego in the mountains above Palm Springs. From there it was 3 1/2 hours across SoCal in pouring rain to hang out with my daughters and some friends before heading back to NorCal.

During that last trip in the rain Bluey developed a stubborn and persistent miss that was eventually traced to not one, but two new distributor caps. Both were black plastic 1942 style crab caps with aluminum wire sockets and contacts. I had installed the first one to replace the red cap that came with the Mallory ignition—because I thought the black cap looked better—before we ever started the engine. Looking back, knowing what I've since learned, I'm surprised that it ran as long and well as it did. But with the Mallory cap in place—brass contacts and no carbon-black electrical paths in the plastic—the motor runs better than it ever has!

HITTING THE TARGET

So, how'd we do with our original plan? Well, we took longer than we should have. The build process covered 22 months and consumed more than 2,000 man-hours. The hour count is much greater than it needs to be because I got a little carried away doing things that didn't have to be done, things like metal polishing and blending

Don Ferrara looks right at home in Bluey's cockpit—and well he should; he was unwittingly responsible for much of the car's design.

welds with parent metal on parts that others will never see—but I know they're there!

Out-of-pocket costs hover somewhere under 20 thou', including plating and upholstery and engine machine work, which were purchased services. All other tasks were done in-house with lots of contributed professional time. Considering that even a mildly built flatmotor can cost more than a new hi-po crate motor from Ford or Chevy, this kind of money for a traditional highboy like Bluey is a bargain. If you're willing to settle for a bit less performance and can get by without a quick-change and top and leather up-

holstery, you could pare several thousand off of the cost and still have a righteous roadster.

Some salient, enduring truths about hot rod building surfaced and were reinforced during the four years of building and enjoying the Bishop-Tardel Highboy: Imagination, thought, experience, care, and focused dedication are all essential to produce first-rate hot rods—just as they always have been.

And good hot rods are built out of love for the work and the automotive treasures it produces, and with lots of freely donated time, energy, and hardware from hot-rodding pals—just as they always have been.

A half-hour up Highway 99 from Bakersfield and this shot, the top got a real workout—for 6 1/2 hours of pouring-down rain, all the way back to the Wine Country and a dry garage.

150

INFORMATION AND PARTS SOURCES

The list of suppliers of parts for traditional Ford hot rods isn't nearly as long as the one for present-tech street rod hardware. Nonetheless, there are enough folks making and selling the hardware you need to build what is essentially a brand new, all-metal, traditional A-V8 roadster. From individual nuts and bolts to brand new bodies, there's no lack of makings for your highboy.

There are more suppliers and resources than those described here, but our list covers the full range of parts and services available and presents both long-time heavy hitters and smaller specialist companies, most of whom we have dealt with first-hand.

The information in the list was accurate at the time the book was published, and with the exception of catalog sizes and prices, we wouldn't expect many changes over a long period of time. Old Ford businesses tend to stay put.

Old Ford technical information is plentiful, accurate, readily accessible, and inexpensive, thanks to the old Ford restoration hobby that grew even as the popularity of old Ford hot rods waned. Most of the technical information is either original material or reprints of Ford-produced "factory" manuals, parts books, and service bulletins.

HISTORY
The American Hot Rod
by Dean Batchelor
This up-close and personal look at the history of the hot rod by the late dean of hot-rodding journalist-authors is great background information for your A-V8 project and a marvelous read. Dean's book is sold through his old friend, hot-rodder and motorbook dealer Neal East at Carbooks, as well as through *Automobile Quarterly* and MBI Publishing Company.

Hot Rod History
by Tex Smith and Tom Medley
Like Montgomery's books, Tex Smith's and Tom Medley's *Hot Rod History* series is based on old photos and first-hand remembrances of early hot-rodders. Not nearly as pictorial as Montgomery's books, they are nonetheless good references for the way things were and the way the cars looked.

Hot Rods of the 1950s
by Andy Southard, Jr.
Many excellent color photos of California hot rods in 1950s-era indoor car shows, drag racing, and just hanging out. Available directly from the renown photographer/painter/striper or through Neal East's Carbooks and MBI Publishing Company.

Don Montgomery's Hot Rod Pictorials
For a detailed look at hot rods from the past you'll want Don Montgomery's first three pictorial histories of hot-rodding in southern California in the 1940s and early 1950s—*HOT RODS IN THE FORTIES: A Blast From the Past, HOT RODS AS THEY WERE: Another Blast From The Past,* and *HOT ROD MEMORIES: Relived Again.* Here you'll find all the neat little tricks and personalizing touches that lent character and individuality to the cars. Montgomery's books can be purchased directly from the author, and they are also sold through MBI Publishing Company, as well as several of the parts suppliers listed.

TECHNICAL
Rebuilding the Famous Ford Flathead
by Ron Bishop
Nostalgia—Rebuilding and Modifying the Flathead Ford V-8
by Ron Holleran.
Tex Smith's The Complete Ford Flathead V-8 Engine Manual
by Ron Ceridono.
These three books are described in Chapter Six and are available directly from the authors, through Neil East's Carbooks, and from MBI Publishing Company.

Ford Green Book
You'll grow to love Ford's Green Book, a great tool for helping you to get the "feel" of old Ford parts. The huge *Ford Chassis Parts and Accessories Catalog* is packed with drawings that will help you identify Ford parts and let you see how they go together in transmissions, rear ends, brakes, steering, and such.

The Green Book also contains application information that tells you which parts will interchange from one year to another.

Reprints of the Green Book, along with other Ford technical books, are available from many Ford parts sources, including All-Ford Parts, Obsolete Ford Parts, Inc., Sacramento Vintage Ford Parts, and Bob Drake.

Ford Service Bulletins, Repair Manuals, and so on

For gearheads accustomed to the corrective Band-Aid approach of modern service bulletins, the Ford service bulletin books look more like an intensive course in Ford mechanical service and repair. Wonderfully thorough and detailed, arranged by major components and systems, each bulletin is a concise lesson in the subject it covers. Each bulletin begins with important specs and moves on to step-by-step instructions for all of the essential tasks. Sad to say, the service bulletins have yet to be reprinted, but they can still be found at swap meets and through Hemmings Motor News.

Catalogs—Your Old Ford Parts and information connection

There's a lot of overlap in parts inventory in the group of suppliers listed, but that's OK because when one is back ordered on a part you need, someone else will probably have it.

PARTS SUPPLIERS

There are many more suppliers than those listed, but these are the heavy hitters. You can find additional sources in *Hemmings Motor News*, but those listed here are ones with whom we have either personal experience or reliable second-hand endorsements and can recommend without question.

All Ford Parts

1600 Dell Ave., Suite A
Campbell, CA 95008
232-page catalog, $10
1-800-532-1932 Order only
1-408-378-1935 Information
1-408-866-1934 FAX
Broad inventory of NOS and quality repro parts—1909 through 1948; extensive accurate illustrations are a big help; competitive prices.

American Stamping Company

P. O. Box 547
Olive Branch, MS 38654
1-601-895-5300 Order and information
Reproduction '32 Ford frame rails.

Brookville Roadster, Inc.

718 Albert Road
Brookville, OH 45309
Catalog, 20 pages, $2
1-937-833-4605 Order and information
Steel Model A roadster and roadster-pickup bodies, beds, windshields, tops, patch panels; Model A frame horns; chassis and body/chassis kits; steel Deuce dashes; assembly and modification services; must-have catalog for A-V8 builders and fans.

Burns Stainless Steel

1013 W. 18th St.
Costa Mesa, CA 92627
1-949-631-5120
Call for catalog
www.burnsstainless.com
Mandrel-bent stainless steel and mild steel tubing U and J bends; straight stainless steel tubing; stainless steel and mild steel collectors.

Carbooks

5138 S. Broadway
Englewood, CO 80110
1-303-762-8595 Order and information
Veteran hot-rodder/journalist Neal East is one of the savviest purveyors of automotive books and magazines; he knows where to find the hard-to-find. Great one-stop shop for getting all the books you need.

Classic Motorbooks

P. O. Box 1
Osceola, WI 54020-0001
1-800-826-6600
1-715-294-4448
Catalog, four per year, free
Thousands of automotive and transportation titles from this largest of automobile book publisher/distributors: Montgomery, Smith/Medley books, among others.

Dennis Carpenter Reproductions

P. O. Box 26398
Charlotte, NC 28221
1-704-786-8139 Information
1-800-476-9653 Order only
F-1, F-100 steering and brake parts; new and rebuilt flathead short blocks.

Coker Tire

1317 Chestnut St.
Chattanooga, TN 37402
1-800-251-6336
Correct vintage-style bias-ply tires; radial wide white-sidewall tires.

Bob Drake Reproductons, Inc.

1819 N. W. Washington Blvd.
Grants Pass, OR 97526
Catalog, 350 pages, $10
1-541-474-0043 Information
1-800-221-3673 Order only

1932–1948 reproduction parts—bright trim to weatherstrip; Ford literature; hardware; wiring, and so on.

The Eastwood Company

231 Shoemaker Road
Pottstown, PA 19464
1-800-345-1178

Restoration tools, paints, finishes; metal-polishing equipment and supplies.

Flathead Jack

1561 Third Ave.
Walnut Creek, CA 94596
Catalog, 64 pages, $16
1-888-932-2233 Order and information
1-510-932-1851 FAX

Full line of flathead rebuild hardware and performance equipment; Isky, Potvin, and Schneider camshafts. Jack handles the phones so be patient if you get a busy signal; talking to him is worth the wait.

The Early Ford V-8 Club

P. O. Box 2122
San Leandro, CA 94577

Write for location of nearest chapter.

Halibrand

P.O. Box 100
500 S. Washington
Wellington, KS 67152
1-800-824-7947

Quick-change rear ends and parts, aluminum wheels, four-spoke steering wheels.

Haneline Products Company

P. O. Box 430
Morongo Valley, CA 92256
Catalog
1-760-363-6597 Order and information
1-760-363-7321 FAX

Complete line of reproduction vintage Stewart-Warner instrument panels; engine-turned facias; vintage Stewart-Warner instruments; outstanding prepurchase support with full-size Xeroxes of panels you are interested in.

Bill Hirsch Automotive

396 Littleton Ave.
Newark, NJ 07103
1-800-828-2061 Order (except NJ)
1-973-642-2404 NJ orders
1-973-642-6161 FAX
hirschauto.aol.com
www.hirschauto.com

Upholstery leather; top fabrics; full line of restoration chemicals, paints.

Ron Holleran

P. O. Box 241
Chester, VT 05143
802-875-2140

The only source we know of for Ron's book: Nostalgia—Rebuilding and Modifying the Flathead Ford V-8. Single copy price $19.95 plus $1.50 for first-class mail (Continental U.S. only; additional for areas outside Continental U.S.); prices subject to change.

Hot Rod & Custom Supply

1304 S. E. 10th St.
Cape Coral, FL 33990
Catalog, 29 pages, $3.50
1-800-741-4687 Order and information
www.rodncustom,com

Tony DiCosta has a full line of flathead parts and speed equipment; good prices.

Joblot Automotive, Inc.

98-11 211th St.
Queens Village, NY 11429
Catalog, 88 pages, $2
1-800-221-0172 Order only (except NY)
1-718-468-8585 Information
(and NY orders)
1-718-468-8686 FAX

NOS and quality repro Ford hard parts specialists; excellent breadth and depth of inventory; lots of hard-to-find pieces; great prices.

Little Dearborn

2424 University Ave. S.E.
Minneapolis, MN 55414
1-612-331-2066

Separate catalogs for Model T, Model A, 1932–1948 Ford, and 1948–1956 Ford pickup, $3 each. Large selection of quality NOS and repro Ford parts, many hard-to-find pieces.

Don Montgomery

Publisher of Hot Rod Books
636 Morro Hills Rd.
Fallbrook, CA 92028
1-619-728-5557
Outstanding pictorial history of 1940s and 1950s
hot rods in southern California and the West.

Motor City Flathead

13624 Stowell Road
Dundee, MI 48131
Catalog, 41 pages, $2.50
1-313-529-3363 Order and information
Flathead rebuild and hop-up parts; full-flow oil
filter system; complete building of stock and
high-performance flathead motors.

PPG Industries

19699 Progress Drive
Twinsville, OH 44136
Check Yellow Pages for name of nearest dealer
Outstanding paint and prep products line; up-to-
the-minute advice.

Roy Nacewicz Enterprises

P. O. Box 285
8032 Allen Road
Allen Park, MI 48101
1-313-383-2692 Order and information
1-313-382-FORD FAX
Fastener catalog for 1932 to 1948 Ford: $3.00 Fas-
tener catalog for Model A Ford: $2.00
The best source of correct Ford fasteners, fittings,
and the other hard-to-find pieces; most items sold
in economical kits; Roy will help you avoid the
"hardware store" or high-tech look on your traditional rod.

Navarro Engineering

4212 Chevy Chase Drive
Los Angeles, CA 90039
Information sheet, free
1-818-241-6644 Order and information
Sole source of Navarro heads and manifolds—
considered by many to be the best; competitive
prices; Barney's still in charge with a telephone
number dating back to the 1940s!

Obsolete Ford Parts, Inc.

8701 S. I-35
Oklahoma City, OK 73149
1-405-631-3933 Information
1-405-634-6815 FAX
Model A catalog, 100 pages, $3
1932–1948 passenger, 1932–1947 pickup, 175
pages, $3
OFP is one of the biggies—broad and deep inventory of NOS and repro parts; competitive prices;
lots of great illustrations in nine catalogs, from
Model Ts to T-Birds; toll-free order-only number
comes with catalog—kinda like a decoder ring.

Patrick's

P. O. Box 10648
Casa Grande, AZ 85230
Catalog, 12 pages, free
1-520-836-1117 Order and information
1-520-836-1104 FAX
Patrick Dykes has a great range of flathead rebuild
and hop-up hardware, geared to traditional rods;
competitive prices; good, knowledgeable service.

Red's Headers

22950 Bednar Lane
Fort Bragg, CA 95437
Catalog, $2
1-707-964-7733 Order and information
E-Mail <info@redheaders.com>
Flathead hardware and speed equipment catalog,
plus a performance guide in which Red Hamilton
shares great flathead hop-up tech tips, photos,
charts.

Sacramento Vintage Ford Parts, Inc.

2484 Mercantile Drive
Rancho Cordova, CA 95742-6200
Model A catalog, $5
V-8 Ford catalog, $5
916-853-2244
916-853-2299 FAX
www.vintage-ford.com
Excellent breadth and depth of Model A and Ford
flathead V-8 hardware; competitive prices and excellent mail-order service.

Scat Enterprises

1400 Kingsdale Ave.
Redondo Beach, CA 90278
1-310-370-5501 Order and information
1-310-214-2285 FAX
NOS Mercury 4.0-inch stroke cranks; custom
ground 4.125-inch strokers.

Joe Smith Automotive, Inc.

2140 Canton Road
Marietta, GA 30066
Catalog, 74 pages, $3.
1-800-235-4013 Order only
1-770-426-9850 Information
1-770-426-9854 FAX
www.joesmithauto.com

Thirty-year history; broad, deep inventory of 1932–1948 NOS and repro parts; lots of catalog illustrations; competitive prices; toll-free order-only number; flathead rebuilding service.

Andy Southard, Jr.

5 San Juan Drive
Salinas, CA 93901-3012

Andy's Hot Rods of the 1950s; 128 pages, soft cover; $19.95 plus $4.50 postage and handling.

SoCal Speed Shop

1357 E. Grand Ave.
Pomona, CA 91766
1-909-469-6171 Order & info
scalspeed@aol.com
www.scalspeedshop.com

New traditional-style shock mounts, headlight stands, hairpins and batwings, and three- and four-spoke steering wheels in stainless.

Southside Obsolete

6819 James Ave. S.
Minneapolis, MN 55423
Catalog, 28 pages
1-612-866-1230 Order and information
1-612-866-8187 FAX

Excellent inventory of important, mostly NOS parts for brakes, suspension, steering, rear end, engine, transmission, electrical; great old Ford illustrations.

Specialty Ford Parts

9103 E. Garvey Ave.
Rosemead, CA 91770
Several catalogs, $6 each
1-626-288-2121 Order and information
1-626-280-4546 Order and information

Catalog 1-92—Stromberg carburetors and hardware; Catalog 2-92—Ford A, B, and C four-banger speed equipment; Catalog 3-92—More Ford four-banger stuff; Catalog 5-92—Flathead V-8 equipment; new catalogs in the works; great hardware and competitive prices; mail order only.

Speedway Motors

P. O. Box 81906
300 Speedway Circle
Lincoln, NE 68501-9896
Catalog, 306 pages, $5
1-402-474-4411 Order and information
1-800-763-3733 FAX

Flathead parts and speed equipment at competitive prices; repro Ford hardware; about 50 pages applicable to old-Ford hot rods.

Stockton Wheel Service

648 W. Fremont St.
Stockton, CA 95203
Catalog
209-464-7771 Order and information
209-464-4725 FAX
www.stocktonwheel.com

All—repeat all—of your Ford hot rod wheel needs can be handled by Frank Mauro's crew, from repair of originals to recreation of new copies, including Kelseys and Ford discs with vented centers.

Vern Tardel Old Ford Parts

464 Pleasant Ave.
Santa Rosa, CA 95401
707-838-6065 FAX only

From our very own Vern Tardel—rear brake drum retainers, reproduction K-members for Model A and Deuce frames, F-1 steering boxes for Model A and Deuce frames, and, of course, the original Stromberg 97 ceramic mug!

Dave Tatom Custom Engines

Vintage Vendors
P. O. Box 2504
Mount Vernon, WA 98273
360-424-8314
360-424-6717 FAX

Dave Tatom is arguably the premiere flathead engine builder today. If you're looking to humble the guys with small block Chevys, Dave's your guy.

U.S. Radiator

6710 Avalon Boulevard
Los Angeles, CA 90003
1-323-778-5390 Order and information
1-323-778-1007 FAX

Deuce style radiators.

BISHOP-TARDEL 1929 FORD ROADSTER SPECS

CHASSIS
1929 Ford frame, stepped rear cross-member,
1932 Ford K-member, 2 1/2-inch drop Mor-Drop axle
1934 Ford wishbone
1940 Ford rear-end, Halibrand V-8 quick-change center
1946 Ford rear radius rods
1948 Ford F-1 steering box
1948 Lincoln brakes

MOTOR
1946 Ford 59A block, ported
1949 Mercury 4-inch crank and rods
Egge 8.5:1 pistons, chrome-moly rings
Isky 400 Jr. cam, valve springs
Johnson adjustable tappets
1.6-inch stainless intake valves, 1.5-inch exhaust
Melling high-volume oil pump
Offenhauser 8.5:1 heads
Offenhauser triple manifold
Three Stromberg 97 carburetors
Stelling & Hellings air cleaners
Custom stainless-steel headers and collectors, Smithy's glasspacks
Mallory dual-point ignition

TRANSMISSION
1939 Ford truck case
1946 Ford passenger car gearset
1939 Ford shifter

BODY
Steel 1929 Ford Standard Roadster by Brookville
2-inch chopped and raked windshield
1932 Ford radiator shell and grille
1950 Pontiac taillights
1936 Ford Washington Blue, PPG Concept

FORD FLATHEAD ENGINE TUNING

SPECS

Firing order

. 1–5–4–8–6–3–7–2

Valve clearance, cold

Intake . . . . . . .1932 to 1948: 0.012 inches
. . . . .1949 to 1953: 0.014 inches
Exhaust . . . . . .1932 to 1948: 0.013 inches
. . . . .1949 to 1953: 0.018 inches

Spark plug

Type . . . . .Champion H-10
Gap . . . . .0.024 inches

Timing

Initial . . . . .6 degrees

Idle speed

. . . . .400–500 rpm

FLUIDS

Engine oil

Grade . . . . .API SF or SG
Viscosity 40W, 20W-50
Capacity . . . . .4 quarts (without filter)

Transmission oil

Grade . . . . .API GL-4
Viscosity . . . . .SAE 140
Capacity . . . . .Fill to bottom of level plug hole

Differential oil—Ford

Grade . . . . .API GL-4
Viscosity . . . . .SAE 140
Capacity . . . . .Fill to bottom of level plug hole

Differential oil—Halibrand

Grade . . . . .API GL-4
Viscosity . . . . .SAE 140
Capacity . . . . .Fill to bottom of level plug hole

Steering lube

. . . . .NLGI No. 2

Cooling system capacity

. . . . .16–18 quarts

INDEX

Ackerman effect, 41
Air filters, 118
Alignment specs, 45
All Ford Parts, 53
American Rodder, 137, 147, 149
American Stamping Company, 32, 33
Andy's Last Picnic, 148
Antique Auto Parts, 110
Assembly area, 20
Assembly, 24
Auburn gauges, 105
Axle-dropping, 35–37
Ayulo, Manuel, 18
B.F.Goodrich, 68
Battery, 123
Bell Auto Parts, 36, 102, 109
Bell midget steering wheel, 102
Beltline reveal, 89
Bendix, 17, 58–60
Bennett, Bob, 14
Bishop, Ron, 21, 70, 71
Bob's Big Boy Drive-In, 148
Body, Filler, 96, 97
Body, Rails, 90
Body, Adjusting, 93, 94
Body, Corrections, 87–89
Body, Magic Adjustment Scheme, 94
Body, Modifications, 90–92
Body, Mounting, 93
Body, Shimming, 93, 94
Body shims, 91
Brake installation guidelines, 59–61
Brake pedal, 104, 105
Brake pedal, Modifying, 62
Brake system, Bleeding, 64
Brake system, Filling, 64
Brake system, Plumbing, 62–64
Brookville Roadster, 86, 87, 90–92, 95
Brown, Charley, 147, 148
Buchanan, Jack, 140

Buggy springs, 46, 47
Bumpsteer, 41, 42, 45
Burns Stainless Steel, 127, 132
California Hot Rod Reunion, 148
Carburetor, Assembly, 115
Carburetor, Cleaning, 114, 115
Carburetor, Corrections, 114, 115
Carburetor, Disassembly, 114, 115
Carburetor, Installation, 115
Carburetor, What to look for, 114
Carburetor, 110
Castetter, John, 144
Catalogs, 21
Catalyzed epoxy primer, 95
Catalyzed primer-surfacer, 97
Ceridono, Ron, 21, 109
Champion, 79
Chandler-Groves carburetor, 110
Channeling, 23
Chasse, Topper, 126
Clutch pedal, 104
Clutch, Selecting, 79
Coker Tire, 68
Column support, 102, 103
Commercial immersion stripping, 95
Cooling system, 79, 80
Cord, 105
Cowl, removing gas tank from, 92
Craft Engine Machine, 53
Cragar, 102
Cross-member, 46, 61–63
Cylinder heads, Selecting, 78
Dago, 36
Dashboard, 92
Deuce dashboard, 106
Deuce frame, 32–34, 90
DiCosta, Tony, 133
Drag link, 43, 45
Drake, Bob, 93
Driveline breakage myth, 15
Driveline, 55–57
Driveshaft, 55, 56
Duesenberg gauges, 105

DuPont epoxy primer, 97
DuPont, 94, 95
Echoff, Bill, 19
Edelbrock, 78, 109, 110
Edwards Air Force Base, 147
El Mirage, 16
Electric fuel pump cutoff switch, 105
Engine work, Cleaning and inspection, 73, 74
Engine work, Grinding and polishing, 74
Engine work, Machining, 74–76
Engines, What to look for, 72, 73
Exhaust port dividers, 76
Exhaust system, 125–133
Exhaust system, Alternate approaches, 132, 133
Exhaust system, fabrication-Choose methods, 128
Exhaust system, Fitting, 129–131
Exhaust system, Mock up, 128
Exhaust system, Normalizing, 131
Exhaust system, Pipes, 133
Exhaust system, Setup, 129
Fan, 79
Ferrara, Don, 7, 9, 35, 93, 125, 132, 137, 148, 149
Firestone Deluxe Champion, 67, 68
Firewall, 92
First Muroc Reunion, 147
Flathead Jack, 77, 116, 117
Flatheadmotor intakes, 108, 109
Flywheel, Selecting, 79
Ford 21A engine, 71, 75
Ford 21-stud flathead, 70, 71
Ford 59A engine, 71, 72, 75
Ford 8BA/CM engine, 71, 72, 75
Ford banjo steering wheels, 103
Ford Flathead, 70–72
Ford Green Book, 21
Ford repair manuals, 21
Ford service bulletins, 21

Frame, Repairing, 25, 26
Frame, Selecting, 25
Front cross-member, 34, 39
Front spring, 38–40
Fuel lines, 117, 118
Fuel pump shutoff switch, 123
Fuel pump, 117
Fuel system, Adjustment, 116–118
Fuel system, Final assembly, 116–118
Fuel tank, 117, 118
Fuse panel, 122
Galamb, Joe, 86
Gearbox, 81, 82
Generator, 120
Grainger, Billy, 94, 137, 144
Griffith, Terry, 120, 122
Grose Jets, 115, 118
Hairpins, 37, 38
Halibrand dummy case, 54
Halibrand Quick-Change parts, 52
Halibrand, 82
Halibrand, Ted, 52
Halloran, Ron, 21
Hand, Bud, 22
Haneline, 106, 107
Hard steering myth, 17
Headlight, Switch, 105, 123
Headlight, Bars, 135, 137
Headlight, Mounts, 134, 135
Helical change gears, 51
Hemmings Motor News, 71
Henshaw, Gary, 137, 148
Hirsch, Bill, 140
Historical references, 21
Holland, Bill, 35, 137
Holleran, Ron, 70
Holley, 110
Hood flange, 91
Hot Rod and Custom Supply, 135
Hot Rod Pictorials, 21
Hot Rod Supply, 133
Hot Rod, 7, 9, 13, 23, 126, 141
Immersion stripping, 95
Ignition, Selelcting, 78, 79
Instruments, 105–107
Interior, 138–140
Interior, Basic guidelines, 139
Interior, Material choices, 139, 140

Interior, Seats and panels, 139
Iskenderian Camsy, 77
JAMCO, 79
Jim Davis Memorial
Goodguys/VRA drags, 147
Jobe, Jere, 109, 110
Johnson adjustable tappet, 75, 77
Jones, Jean, 24
Kelsey-Hayes wire wheels, 64–66
K-member, 1932 Ford, 27–29, 31–34, 61, 62, 103, 104
L.A. Roadsters Show, 147
LaSalle transmission, 81
Leaf spring, 37
Lee, Bob, 141, 142
Letherman, Walt, 129
Lights, 120
Lincoln-Zephyr, 82
Lowe, Jack, 149
Lubriplate, 85
Magic Body-Adjustment Scheme, 94
Magnaflux, 72–74
Magnum, 36
Mallory, 78, 79
Master cylinder bracket, 63
Master cylinder, 62
Master cylinder, Installation, 62
Medley, Tom, 148
Metallic filler, 96
Meyer, Eddie, 109
Mitchell, Dave, 101, 126
Mojave Timing Association, 22
Montgomery, Don, 21, 23, 141
Mor-Drop, 36
Motor mounts, 26, 27
Mufflers, 133
Muroc Reunion, 147
Nacewickz, Joe, 85
NAPA, 118
Naugahyde, 138–140
Navarro, Barney, 78
Nostalgia—Rebuilding and Modifying the Flathead Ford V-8, 21, 70
Oakland Roadster Show, 144–146
OEM Ford wheels, 66
Offenhauser, 78, 109, 116, 117, 135
Oil pump, Selecting, 76

Optima II battery, 123
Overheating myth, 15
Paint, 94–100
Paint, Applying color, 99
Paint, Buying Services, 100
Paint, Color sanding, 99
Paint, Polishing, 99
Painting safety tips, 97
Parking brake, 64
Parks, Wally, 13
Parts storage, 20
Patrick's, 78, 79, 116
Pedal assembly, 104
Pedals, 103–105
Personalizing your hot rod, 21, 23, 24
Pinion bearing cage, 50
Pirelli tires, 139
Pistons, Selecting, 76
Pitman arm, 45
Poor brakes myth, 15
Potvin, 77
PPG NCP 271 primer-surfacer, 97
PPG, 94, 95
Primer, 95
Project plan, 17
Project space required, 17
Project time required, 17
Race motor crankshaft, 77
Radiator shell, 91, 92
Radiator, 79
Radius rods, 47, 48
Rear axle, 49–55
Rear axle bearing races, 53
Rear axle, Ford banjo, 49
Rear axle, Halibrand Quick-Change, 49–53
Rear body rails, 89
Rear cross-member, 28, 30–34, 46, 48, 91
Rear spring, 46
Rear spring, Tailoring and trimming, 47
Rear trunk skirt, 91
Rear-end banjo, 46, 47
Rear-wheel bearing races, 53
Rebuilding the Famous Ford Flathead, 21, 70
Red's Headers, 77

Regulator, 120
Rod, 42
Rolland, Bill, 9, 125, 132
Russell, Mike, 149
Safety hub retainer block, 53, 55
Safety hubs, 53, 55
Schank, Terry, 131
Scotch-Brite, 95
Sealed Power piston rings, 77
Sears Point Raceway, 147, 148
Seat frame, 92
Services required, 20, 21
Sexton, Rod, 128, 129
Shifter, 104
Shinoda, Larry, 12
Shock absorber mounts, 42, 133, 134
Shock absorbers, 42, 48
Shock mounts, 42
Shocks, 42
Smith, Mark, 16
Smith, Tex, 21, 70, 71, 109, 110
Smithy's Mufflers, 131, 133
Solenoid, 122
Specialty Ford Parts, 47, 64, 79
Speedway Motors, 32, 41, 53, 135
Spindles, 38, 41
Spline adapter, 56
Split wishbone, 37, 38
Spring hangers, 48
Spring hangers, Deuce frame, 47
Spring hangers, Model A frame, 47
Spring perches, 40

Spruce body shims, 91
Starter button, 105, 123
Starter solenoid, 123
Starter, 120
Steering arm, 38, 41, 42
Steering box, Making it fit, 44, 45
Steering column, 102–104
Steering, 42–45
Steering, Inspection, 44
Steering, Rebuilding, 44
Steering, Service, 44
Steering, What to look for, 43, 44
Stewart, Bob, 36, 149
Stewart, Ed "Axle", 36, 149
Stewart-Warner Sports Panel, 106
Stroker McGurk, 148
Stromberg carburetors, 109–114, 116, 117
Surface preparation, 97–99
Surface preparation, Applying filler, 97
Surface preparation, Applying primer-surfacer, 98, 99
Surface preparation, Applying putty, 98
Surface preparation, Materials, 97
Surface preparation, Technique, 97
Surface preparation, Tools, 97
Taillights, 92, 93
Tardel drum retainer, 54, 55
Tardel, Vern, 7, 21, 24, 28, 32, 53, 55, 80, 82, 137, 143, 144, 146, 147, 149

Tattersfield intake manifold, 109
Technical references, 21
The Complete Ford Flathead V-8 Engine Manual, 21, 70, 109
Thickstun intake manifold, 109
Throttle linkage, 115, 116
Throttle linkage, Three-carb installation, 116
Throttle linkage, Two-carb installation, 115, 116
Throttle pedal, 105
Tires, 66–68
Tools required, 20
Top, 141, 142
Torque tube, 56, 126
Transmission, Assembly, 85
Transmission, Disassembly, 83
Transmission, Inspection, 83
Transmission, Installation, 85
Transmission, Parts, 84
Transmission, What to look for, 82, 83
Valvetrain, Selecting, 77
Voltage regulator, 120
Water pumps, 79
Wheels, 64–66
Wheels, Ford, 65, 66
Where to find parts, 13, 15
Williams, Bill, 7
Windshield posts, 136, 137
Wiring, 120–122
Wishbone, 37
Workbench, 20